Prais

"*Blood Sisters* is both funny and profoundly sad at the same time. This remarkable memoir shows how child abuse can happen almost in plain sight and how children suffer when those who can help choose to look the other way. For child welfare professionals *Blood Sisters* should serve as a reminder of our responsibilities. Children like Betsy are counting on us."

—Tim Brandau, Ph.D, Executive Director, Child, Inc.

"*Blood Sisters* was already a deeply felt, original memoir when Billie Travalini began it at the Temple University graduate program in creative writing and it is even more powerful a story now. Her writing is stunning; her handling of the now familiar themes of incest and child abuse so graceful and haunting it's as if we have never read about these subjects before. Especially unique is the quality of solidarity among victims, a truth that too few writers have accessed."

—Joan Mellen, author of *A Farewell to Justice* and *The Great Game in Cuba*

"Billie Travalini's story could be told anywhere, and yet she makes it her own. *Blood Sisters* is a smart and lively read about the power of sisterhood, the resilience of two, and the unbreakable bonds of love."

—Cecilia Galante, author of *The Patron Saint of Butterflies*

"If Billie Travalini's expanded memoir, *Blood Sisters*, tells the reader anything, it's that an emotionally and sexually abused child is as multidimensional as one lucky enough to have a relatively happy childhood. The story flows effortlessly from the mind of a 12-year-old to create an intense and compellingly detailed world studded with childlike games, southern humor, and relationships with siblings, parents and friends. Travalini portrays the abuse in a wider, richer context—a tribute to both her power as a writer and as a survivor."

—Victor Greto, freelance journalist and professor at Wesley College

"As gripping as it is timeless, *Blood Sisters* is the story of Betsy Toppin, a precocious 10-year-old physically and sexually abused by her biological father, as society turns a blind eye...a must-read for anyone who cares about the rights of children."

—Debra Kirsh, RN, BSN, MJ, PHRN

Jim Gilmore

About the Author

Billie Travalini's work has appeared in *Another Chicago Magazine, Revue Review, The Moth, Writers on Writing: The Art of the Short Story,* the *Journal of Caribbean Literatures,* and *Gargoyle,* among others. An earlier version of *Blood Sisters,* titled *Bloodsisters,* was a finalist for the Bakeless Literary Prize and James Jones Award, and won the Lewis Clark Discovery Prize. Her other books include *No Place Like Here: An Anthology of Southern Delaware Poetry and Prose,* 2012; *Teaching Troubled Youth: A Practical Pedagogical Approach,* 2008; and *On the Mason-Dixon Line: An Anthology of Contemporary Delaware Writers,* edited with Fleda Brown, 2008. She has received fellowships in poetry and fiction from the Delaware Division of the Arts, teaches at Wilmington University, coordinates the Lewes Creative Writers' Conference, and is a popular workshop leader and presenter. An advocate for troubled youth and the mentally ill, she lives in Wilmington, Delaware, where she is busy at work on *Independence Day,* a short story collection, and *Sunshine,* a sequel to *Blood Sisters.*

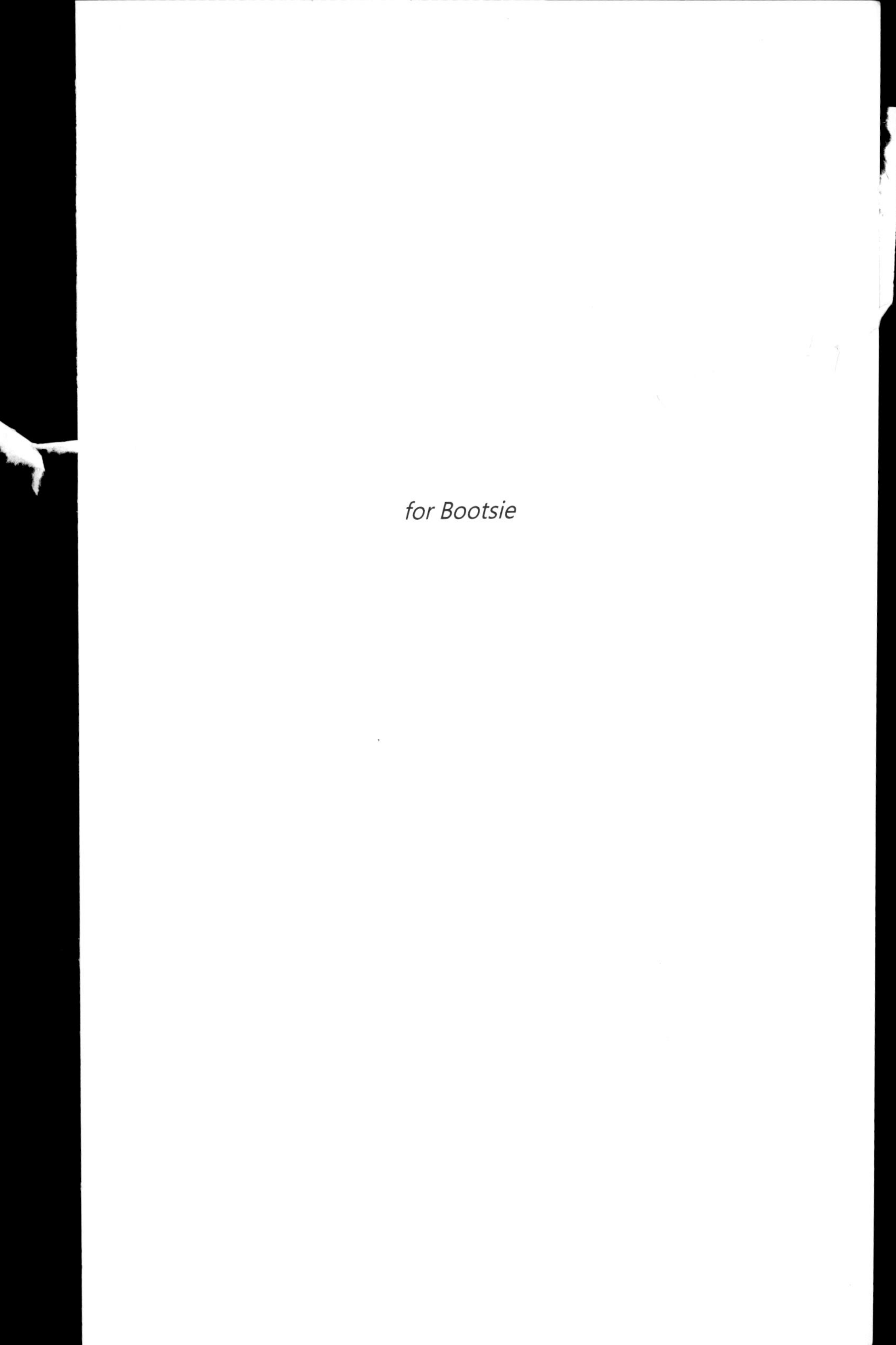

for Bootsie

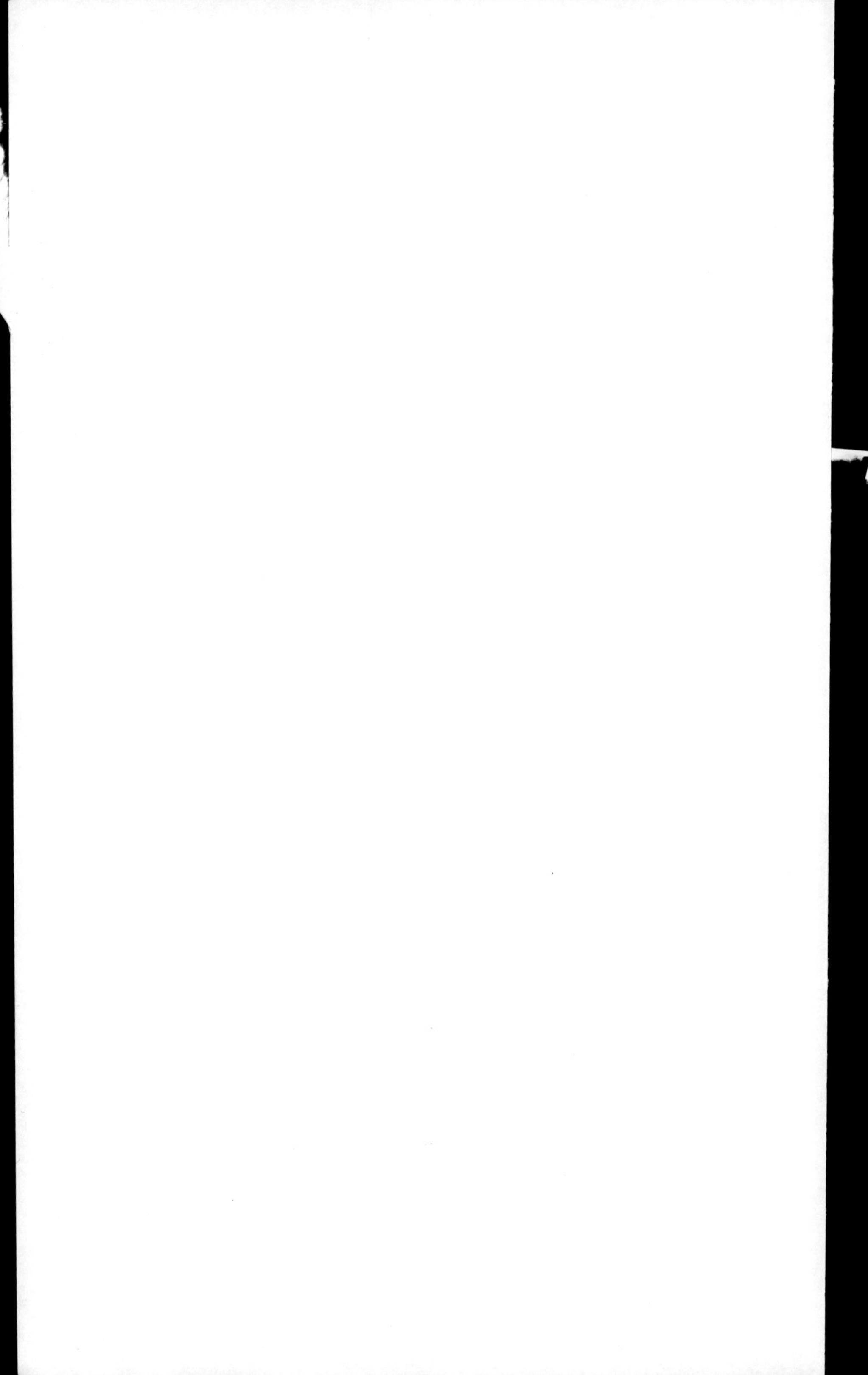

BLOOD SISTERS

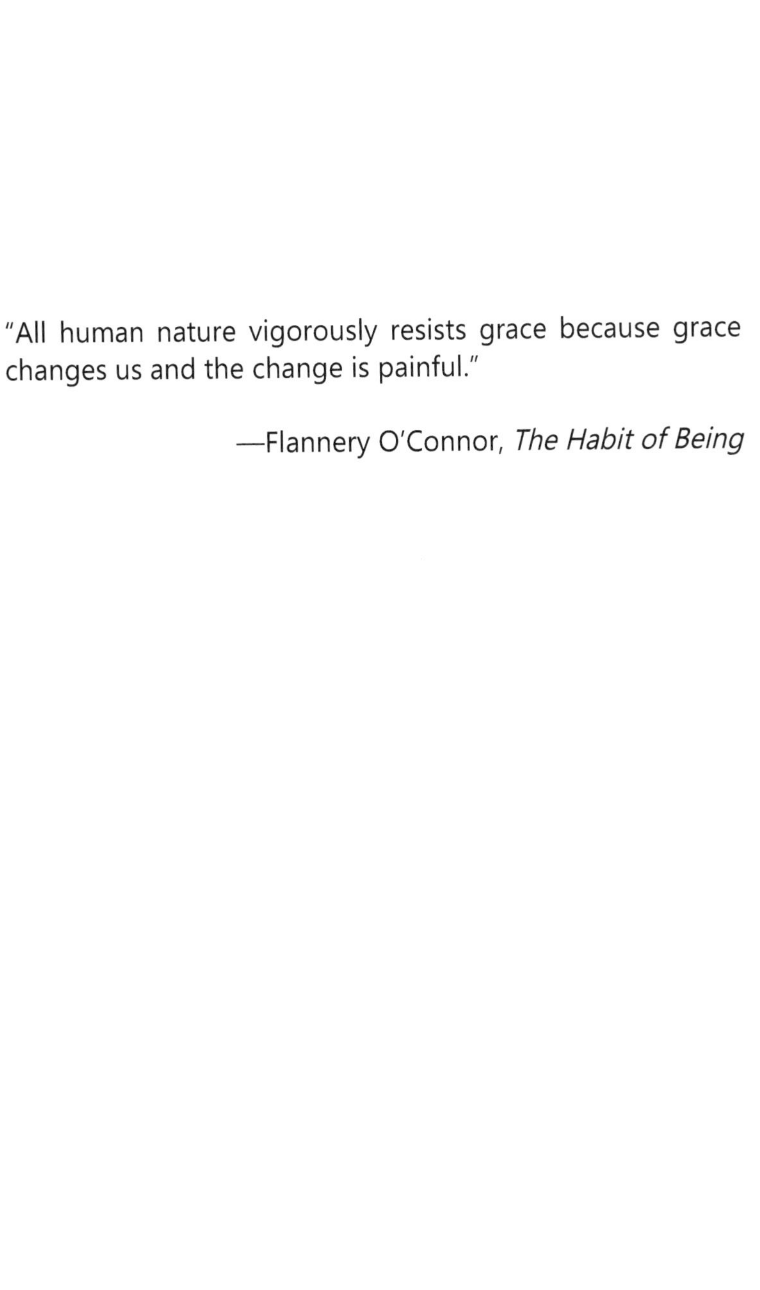

"All human nature vigorously resists grace because grace changes us and the change is painful."

—Flannery O'Connor, *The Habit of Being*

Contents

With thanks to James O'Neill Miller, whose poetic eye was relentless in its search for *more*; to Abby Millager and Doll's Eye Press for giving me great advice and a great cover; and a special thanks to my home state of Delaware, where the North and South meet in some mighty interesting ways and a scrappy, unwanted kid can find what she needs to build a full and happy life.

I

Homecoming

Wilmington, Delaware
Summer, 1960

The driver's name was Woody Hicks. He lived next door to my real mother and my real father. The garbage truck we were riding in was his. And I was going home. None of which pleased me.

"The missus sure seems nice." The driver didn't know Mama Cope and I resented his sliding in some comment like he did. I pushed myself closer to the door and stroked Sissy Jupe's big, orange head. "My pretty kitty," I said, cutting him off. Sissy was sleeping in the folds of my pinafore, hiding the pink tulips that Mama Cope had embroidered into the shape of a heart. Mama Cope was my foster mother. When she put my suitcase on the seat next to the driver, she straightened my ponytail with her long, soft fingers. Then she told me to be good and promise I wouldn't be so stubborn. I did, but she knew I was hopeless so she just gathered me up in her arms and laughed.

"Just don't go getting yourself in any trouble," she said, pulling a hankie out of her pocket and dusting the tops of my new pink leather shoes. "I hope to visit real soon." Then she let go and I could see her eyes filling up with tears.

That was two years ago. I was ten. And before my real parents came into the picture, I was happy. Mama Cope had raised me from the time I was two months old and we had gotten used to each other. Her husband, James, died when I was three. I don't remember him much, except that he was a quiet man and smoked fat, smelly cigars from a can.

After he died, Mama Cope did her best to bring me up right. She taught me how to garden and talk to Jesus and make cutout snowflakes from tissue paper.

Suddenly I was supposed to forget all that. Give it all up as if it were nothing more than a big balloon with the air sucked out. Gone. And all I could see I had for it was a ride in a smelly garbage truck and Mama Cope's sweet face looking after me as we pulled away. When we were almost out of sight, I saw her pick a marigold from her garden and wave it above her head. I didn't wave back. I wanted to, but I didn't. Waving was too much like saying good-bye for good. So I leaned my face to the window and watched Mama Cope fade from view like a passing road sign. Then everything was gone. The red maple tree she and I grew from a seedling, the metal rooster standing on the roof pecking at the wind, even the pale chalk lines of my last hopscotch game. I remembered how Rita Rosini and I had been playing in the street with the sun beating down on our bare shoulders. As usual, I won. Rita had as much coordination as a cow. And that's the truth. But we both collected baseball cards and liked Nancy Drew mysteries. I would've liked her even more if she hadn't been such a big bragger. I never had much use for braggers, but I made an exception in Rita's case because she loved baseball almost as much as I did. Before moving to Delaware she lived in the Bronx, one block from Yankee Stadium. There, she said, statues of ballplayers like Babe Ruth and Lou Gehrig stood at every intersection and if she opened her bedroom window she could hear the announcer's voice almost as clearly as if she were sitting behind home plate. The Yankees was my team—reliable, handsome—and, I didn't even mind when Rita got some of the details mixed up and moved the stadium to Brooklyn and Lou Gehrig's statue over to where Babe Ruth's had been. Rita was different than most braggers. She had a soft heart. When she learned I was moving she gave me every one of her baseball cards. Even her Mickey Mantle and Roger Maris cards.

I was thinking about all this, when what happens but I catch a glimpse of Rita in her mother's station wagon. I ducked because the last thing in the world I wanted was for them to see me riding in a garbage truck. Even so, I had to fight the urge to take one more look around. I don't know why, but I had this terrible fear that I had to hold on to every last detail or one day I might start to forget who I am. And I vowed I would never let that happen, no matter what.

"Couldn't help noticing your cat's blind," the driver said. He was puffing on a Lucky Strike, which hung from his lip, cowboy style. He steered with both hands, letting the ash fall onto his lap, then brushing it off every so often without taking his eyes off the road. "Got a glass eye myself."

I didn't answer, but he was saying all the right stuff. I couldn't help being interested. I rested my feet on the metal hump in the floor over the engine and twisted sideways. His eye looked real enough, though it didn't move at all. Just sat there. Like a pale blue star with its light almost gone. I kept hoping it wouldn't fall out.

"Mighty healthy-looking cat," he said, between puffs. I noticed that his voice was softer than his face, which was the color and texture of worn leather. But it was a nice face, and his glass eye, smooth as a robin's egg, gave it character. Every now and then I would check his eye to make sure it was where it was supposed to be.

Sometimes, when I was checking, I almost said something. Once I was about to call him Woody, but I caught myself. I reasoned that if I let my guard down, my memory might go soft and I might change into somebody I didn't even know. I saw it happen on *Wagon Train*. An Indian boy went to live with white folks and, in no time flat, he forgot all about being Indian.

I put Sissy's face to the window so he could see what was going on. Of course he couldn't see because his eyes didn't have pupils and light bounced off of them like two colored mirrors. Even so, I liked pointing things out to him.

"Motorcycle, boy," I said.

"Guess you thought you had yourself a girl cat when you named him," the driver laughed.

I wasn't about to let myself get trapped into a long conversation, so I directed my words at the half-closed window. No way, I mouthed.

We drove onto a two-lane highway. I was bored so I unzipped the front pocket on my suitcase and slid my hand in. The pocket was deep and I had to push aside a pile of baseball cards to find what I was looking for.

"Finally," I said, and opened a small book to page two twenty-three. There, smooth and pretty as a store-bought hankie, was the last tissue snowflake that Mama Cope made me. It was pink and had a house in the center and lots of flowers around the edges. I was about to read, but I reminded myself that I needed to study my surroundings. I put my book back and stared out the window.

The driver threw me a glance. "What's your book called?"

"*Hard Times,*" I mumbled. I could've said how the man that wrote Scrooge wrote it and how Mama Cope read it to me and how it's hard to read, but I didn't. I could've also said how Sissy Jupe, a smart circus girl, is in the book, and that would've cleared up his question about my cat's name. But I didn't mention that either. Instead, I kept staring out the window.

It stayed quiet for a long while. Then the driver pulled his cigarette from his lip and his voice came back.

"Feel free to roll your window down more," he said, throwing his cigarette out. "Gets pretty hot in here."

He didn't mention the smell. I thought about how when somebody farts, they look around hoping they're the only one who can smell it. Of course, they aren't. Even so, Mama Cope said it's good to let them think so. I reasoned the same kind of thinking applied to this situation. So I lowered my window and stretched my arm across the empty space.

"Better?" I said, and rested Sissy Jupe's chin on my arm.

We were in the center of a big town and it sort of looked familiar and it sort of didn't. The town had a Warner movie theater and a Woolworth's and an old train station with fancy brickwork and high windows. When we passed something interesting, I pointed Sissy's head in the right direction and explained what we were looking at.

The driver signaled to the left and we turned onto a one-way street. Along the curb farmers, with straw hats pulled down over their eyes, sat in the backs of pickup trucks, shouting: "Chickens. Come get ya fresh chickens." Up the block were the corn farmers and they were shouting, too, and so was the egg man, and the string-bean man and the string-bean man's wife. She was real fat and was holding up fistfuls of beans, smiling.

"Ever been to Wilmington before?" The driver's voice was a lot stronger with the cigarette gone.

I wasn't sure, but I shook my head, no, just the same.

"Well, on Friday and Saturday farmers drive up from Kent and Sussex, and sell just about anything. I don't see him today, but one fella carves fruit out of wood. Mrs. Hicks bought a bunch and Boy Boy, he's my son, almost lost a tooth on an apple one night."

It seemed to me that only idiots and blind people would buy fruit you can't eat. Even so, I appreciated the information, so I nodded my thanks and mumbled, "Dumb."

"Can't deny that," the driver laughed.

As we moved up the street a ways, the farmers were replaced by men selling ice cream from metal boxes strapped to their chests. I saw a clown, too. He had orange hair and baggy pants and giant balloons tied around one hand. I stuck my head out the window to get a better look. Suddenly, I smelled something good.

"Fresh-roasted," the driver said.

As I pulled in the aroma, I studied passersby, determined to find the source.

"Over there on the corner," the driver said, excitedly.

My eyes nearly fell out of my head.

"Holy cow, Sissy, a real peanut man." I was staring at a six-foot burlap peanut, shouting, "Peanuts. Get ya fresh-roasted peanuts."

"Outfit must get pretty hot," the driver said, slowing down. "Think we oughta buy some and help the fellow out?"

"No thank you."

The driver called the peanut man over and bought a bag just the same. Then he cracked a few and threw the shells out the window.

"Sure you don't want any?" He waited for my reply, then popped the peanuts in his mouth.

Slowly, the truck started moving again, then stopped unexpectedly.

"Women can't park to save their lives."

I looked through the front windshield just in time to see a green Chevy jump the curb and hit a parking meter. The driver looked a lot like Sister Catherine, my third grade teacher, only she wasn't wearing nun clothes and had a frown on her face.

"Had enough space for ten cars," the driver said, moving down the street.

"Look Sissy, a circus poster."

"An awful lot of folks are going." Suddenly, it occurred to me that the driver's voice sounded genuine. I was glad because people with phony-sounding voices always get on my nerves. The social worker who told me I had to live with my real mother and father and how it was all for the best had a voice like that. Her name was Miss Reinheart. She had the phoniest voice in the whole world. I hated it.

I turned so Sissy Jupe was facing the driver, then I said: "We love the circus, don't we?"

After a long pause, as if he was sorting out something important in his head, the driver said: "You and Mister Jupe make quite a pair.

"Sissy Jupe," I corrected.

"I'm not sure cats are allowed, but I overheard Bill and Virginia talking about going to the circus. Don't quote me on that, though."

Bill and Virginia were my parents, but it sounded funny hearing them referred to by their first names. Mama Cope had always called them "your real mother and father" and Miss Reinheart would say "Mr. and Mrs. Toppin." I figured it was her way of reminding me that I had their last name and that was supposed to mean something. Of course, it didn't.

When the light changed, the driver pulled over to the curb and got out. I watched him walk over to the poster and catch his thumbnail under the staples and pop them out one by one. Then he tucked the poster under his arm and got back in his truck.

"Thought you might like to have this," he said.

"Thank you." I might have said more but I was too shocked and impressed to keep a record of it. I never saw anyone take something in plain sight like that, snatch it as casually as if he were picking an apple off his own tree, as if he had every right in the world to it. It raised my opinion of him, considerably.

When he handed me the poster I did another quick-check of his eye, without him spotting me. I felt a little guilty since he was trying hard to be nice. Besides, Mama Cope said people with glass eyes and missing legs don't like you staring at them, so I gave him a little smile and lowered my head.

Anyway, that's when I noticed, for the first time, the leather belt wrapped around his waist. The belt was as thin as a lasso and spun through his belt loops two or three times, until only a foot or so was tied off in front like a double-laced boot. All of a sudden it occurred to me that the driver was a poor person. And, since he lived next door to my parents, I wondered if they were poor too, and, if they were, did they wrap their belts and drive a smelly garbage truck.

"Bill have a car?" I blurted out. Mama Cope had a thing against children calling elders by their first name, but I had a feeling the driver was different. He hesitated a moment, then said: "Ford wagon. Broke down or they would've come and got you themselves.

"Hope they disappear," I thought, standing the poster on one leg. "King the Lion, Brooks International Circus, Thursday through Saturday Only," I read aloud.

"Might want to show Carole and Bootsie," the driver said.

I kept my eyes on the poster. The truth is I couldn't have moved if I had wanted to. My insides froze up. I had forgotten all about having sisters. Mama Cope had told me about them, but I didn't know them any better than I knew my real parents, which is saying I didn't know them. I only met all four once. Miss Reinheart made the arrangements shortly after Mama Cope petitioned the court to adopt me. Mama Cope said being I was ten, it was time we made things legal between us. Betsy Cope. I reasoned if I had her last name, I would be her daughter for keeps, and my real mother and father couldn't show up and ruin things.

It was a sound plan but just when I was accepting my new sense of permanence, I learned that being adopted was hard work. Mama Cope explained how we had to go to family court in person so a judge could decide if she could keep me. I told her straight out I had a bad feeling about the whole thing. It seemed to me that talking to a judge would only complicate things. After all, I said, he didn't know a single thing about us that he hadn't heard second hand. Mama Cope said my faith was sagging and things would work out. I decided to take her word for it because I knew I wouldn't have a moment's peace if I believed otherwise.

That May a judge finally found the time to see us. We all met in a big courtroom. The room had a high ceiling and a marble floor the color of cooked shrimp. The judge's bench was the same color only it had a lot of dark veins in it like the tops of old people's hands. The judge was fat-faced and had Miss Reinheart's eyes. He sat behind all that marble like an old king on a throne. I grabbed a piece of Mama Cope's dress and didn't let go. Every so often she would give my arm a little pat to calm my jitters. It worked, too. Once the judge starting talking, things proceeded pretty quickly. I tried hard to keep on track. And I did right up until Miss Reinheart and the judge starting throwing around a lot of big, legal-sounding words I didn't understand.

I used those occasions to look over my real mother and father. It felt strange, like staring at strangers at the supermarket and thinking you might know them and you might not. My father had an old face and wide shoulders and, except for a tattoo of a rose just above his right elbow, he was plain looking. What was left of his hair was brown. He didn't have my nose, my chin, my lips, nothing. He noticed my gaze and returned it with a dimestore smile. The smile was stiff and looked forced and made his cheeks and lips lift up unnaturally. His eyes were as black as a crow's eyes and stuck in my mind. I felt Mama Cope's dress ball up in my hand and my fingers squeeze into a fist. Taking a deep breath, I reminded myself to hold onto my faith like she told me to. That's when I heard Miss Reinheart say: "Your Honor, Mr. Toppin is now gainfully employed and I have a medical report stating that Mrs. Toppin has regained her health; therefore, it is the position of the Children's Bureau that the natural parents be given full permanent custody."

Slowly I turned and looked at my mother. She was a short, slim woman and wore a white dress with tiny red roses on it. Her hair was a pretty auburn color and shiny. I studied her for quite awhile before she returned the attention. When she did, she looked at me with eyes that were soft and sad looking. Then she glanced over her shoulder at Carole and Bootsie and slowly turned her eyes back on me before pointing them at the judge. Carole and Bootsie were skinny and had my father's plain looks. I could tell by their bored expressions that they didn't want to be there any more than I did.

When the judge and Miss Reinheart were done, my father spoke. Seems he was willing to give me up, but my mother said: "Blood is blood. Can't change that by turning our daughter over to some stranger to be raised."

I heard my mother tell the old, fat-faced judge those exact words. Then I saw the judge nod his head as if what she was saying made perfectly good sense. "In the best interest of the child," the judge concluded, "effective as of June 1, 1960, I am granting the natural parents, William Henry and Virginia Ann Toppin, full and permanent custody of Billie Elizabeth Toppin, also known as Betsy Toppin. I further order that all contact with the foster mother, Rebecca Cope, be terminated." When he was done, I saw Miss Reinheart's skinny lips part in a smile and Mama Cope crying. My father was smiling, too, a real big smile that came out through his eyes.

Slowly the scene faded and, in the back of my head, Mama Cope was holding that picked marigold in the air, waving.

My eyes started watering. The driver was looking straight ahead, but I knew he was watching me with his good eye. The way he kept cocking his head to the side gave him away. But he had sense enough to keep quiet and I was grateful for that. I stroked Sissy Jupe a few times to settle myself. I wasn't much for crying. Mama Cope said it had to do with me being stubborn. I saw Mama Cope cry twice: when the fat-faced judge gave his ruling and when Woody Hicks showed up in his garbage truck. They were the two worst days of my life.

"Almost there," the driver said.

We were on a four-lane highway. There was a Goodyear Tire store and a Texaco gas station on one side and a Gulf station and some houses with tall hedges on the other. When the houses ended, there was a big empty field and, in the distance, on the top of a high hill, I could see a large brick building.

"Veterans Hospital," the driver offered. "When it snows, good place for sledding."

I didn't plan to stick around long enough to see snow. We drove a little ways more, and then turned off the highway onto a side street. The street was marked by a steel pole with a rusted sign that read, "Brighton Avenue." A brick house with a bakery sign on the lawn sat behind the pole. The bakery didn't have a large window for displaying creampuffs and cakes and lemon meringue pies like "Nappi's." Nappi's was my favorite bakery and when I was good Mama Cope took me there and let me pick whatever I wanted. I always got a creampuff.

Brighton Avenue was long and skinny and had a drainage ditch down one side. The driver was riding the brake, as if he was expecting some sort of danger ahead. I eyed the street closely. It was full of potholes and, in between the potholes, there were lots of stones with pieces of glass and dirt mixed in.

"You ever need anything, anything at all, you come see me," I heard the driver say.

On both sides of the street narrow houses were bunched together in rows like seats in a movie theater. The houses all looked the same, white with high front steps and porches. On the porches, sitting in wooden rockers, or leaning on stair railings, I saw plain-looking women talking to tired-looking men. Children, wearing T-shirts and no shoes were jumping rope, laughing. Suddenly I realized this was what Mama Cope was talking about when she said: "Everybody doesn't live the way we do, people have their own ways of doing things."

The more I saw the more worried I got. Then, from out of nowhere, a stucco house came into view. The house had a large, horseshoe driveway edged with all sorts of pretty flowers.

"Snapdragons," I said, pointing Sissy's face at the window.

"That's the Benson house," the driver said. "They got two girls, Sarah and Jean Ann. Their daddy works for the state and does all right for himself."

I thought about quizzing him about the girls' ages, but I decided against it. Instead, I mumbled, "We still in Delaware?"

"Didn't even leave New Castle County. You're used to the country. This was country, too, before the city started creeping up on us."

I thought about Mama Cope's house. First, I saw the whole thing. The lace curtains. The rooster sitting on the roof pecking at the wind. The brass doorknocker shaped like a pineapple. The garden. Then I saw Mama Cope waving that picked marigold. I couldn't get that picture out of my head no matter what.

"I'm leaving," I said, firmly. It was a lie, but the truth didn't make much sense, so I had to tell myself a few lies to straighten out everything in my head.

"Well, Betsy," the driver said, calling me by my name. "I hope you won't leave before you give us a chance to get to know you."

I lowered my eyes, without answering. "My pretty kitty," I said, stroking Sissy Jupe's head.

Suddenly, I felt the truck jerk forward and come to a full stop. I looked up. On the driver's side was a big empty lot with junk cars at one end.

"Home," the driver said, pointing out my window to the ugliest house on the whole street. The paint was peeling and giant, ugly weeds had taken over the front yard. Sitting alongside the curb was a red Ford with one wheel missing and white letters on the side that read, "William H. Toppin Home Improvement, Inc."

"Looky," the driver said, turning sideways to see better. "Everyone's on the porch. The tall one's my missus and that's my son, Boy Boy next to her. I reckon you know the others." He took a long pause, then added, "Quite a welcome."

I told him I already had a home.

He opened his mouth to speak but no words came out. I followed his eyes out the window and found myself staring point-blank at my father. He was leaning on the railing and his crow-like eyes were locked on mine. I swallowed hard and studied the rest of his face. He was still wearing a dimestore smile and I tried to work up a smile of my own but I couldn't. Every time I went to part my lips, they stuck to my teeth and my eyes dropped in a squint. I wanted

Mama Cope. I wanted her to tell me I was going to be fine, although I knew by the look on my father's face, I wasn't. Even so, I longed to hear the sound of her voice. I would've given away every one of my baseball cards if I could've heard her right then. But the only voice I heard was the driver's.

"Remember, you ever need anything, you come see me." He was trying to cheer me up, but seeing my father again took the wind right out of me.

Standing on one side of my father was Mrs. Hicks. She was as big as a man and wore her hair in a tiny bun at the nape of her neck and gold, wire-rimmed glasses. She reminded me of the Amish women in Dover who sell homemade jelly and pies at the Farmers Market, only she didn't wear a white doily on her head.

When I was done with her I swept my eyes over the whole bunch of them. I noticed that they were dressed poor and stood with their heads lowered a bit like once a year churchgoers. The sight of them made my stomach drop. Mama Cope said it's no sin being poor but I wondered how I was supposed to act now that I was one of them, being I lacked experience in such matters. From the looks on their faces, I assumed that being poor made people frown—nervous frowns—the kind people wear to the dentist. After a moment, cautious smiles came onto their faces and got mixed in with their frowns. My mother waved at me and the rest of them did the same.

"Time to get out," the driver said.

"Nooooo." I was looking at my father. His smile was bigger than any of the others. Even so, I had a strong feeling that he didn't like me. I don't know why, but I did.

"Hold onto Mister Jupe," the driver said in a gentle voice. "It's a big step down."

"Sissy Jupe," I corrected. Then I pushed the heavy truck door open and half slid and half stepped onto the street.

I'm leaving, I said over and over in my head. I said it until my brain got tired and I saw my mother walking towards me with a sad, childlike smile on her face. She was wearing the white dress with the roses on it and high-heeled shoes. When she was just a foot or two away, her eyes dropped and she paused a moment, the way Mama Cope did when she put my suitcase on the seat next to the driver. Suddenly a sense of panic came over me. I felt tears, hot, heavy ones, trying hard to get out, but I didn't let them. I wrapped my arms around Sissy Jupe and followed my mother to the porch and slowly went inside.

II

Being Stubborn Helps

When Mama Cope said I was stubborn she was telling the truth. I never was the sort of person who goes along with something without asking a fistful of questions. Most of them stay inside my head. But what seems to bother some people is that while I'm asking a question inside my head, I'm not doing whatever it is they think I should be doing. Take when I was in the first grade. I had these twins in my class, Don and Donna Callahan. They had orange hair and freckles and my teacher, Mrs. Frost, loved them to death. Anyway, one day Mrs. Frost told everybody to draw a turtle. I tried, as best as I could, to come up with one good reason why she would suddenly need twenty-eight pictures of turtles. I couldn't think of any though, so there I sat staring out the window, confused. Well, the next thing I knew Mrs. Frost was pushing my desk and yelling. At first I couldn't get what she was saying, but when she started yanking on my arms, my ears cleared up just fine. She thought I was about to copy Don Callahan's turtle. I tried to tell her I wasn't, but the truth only made things worse. She called me a liar and ordered me to stand in the hall. Of course, I refused. So she yanked on my arms some more, and asked the class to indicate, with a show of hands, how many had witnessed my alleged transgression. Nobody raised a hand for the longest time.

Then Mrs. Frost went into a long-winded lecture on the virtue of honesty and Don and Donna Callahan caved in, simultaneously. Mrs. Frost thanked them a million times for being such good examples. Donna leaned towards me, smirking.

"Liar," I said, gripping the sides of my desk.

Mrs. Frost cocked her head and stared me eye to eye. Her face looked real wrinkled and she smelled like a wet towel that's been sitting too long. I wanted to vomit.

"Get away." I could feel tears trying to come out, but I didn't let them.

"We'll see about this." Mrs. Frost was about one hundred years old, but she was strong. She gave my arms another yank, then went straight for the door.

As soon as she disappeared into the hall, I rubbed my skin to get the blood moving again. Then I looked up and saw Mrs. Frost coming through the door with the second grade teacher, Mrs. Lang, in tow. They each grabbed an arm. But I could tell by the look on Mrs. Lang's face her heart wasn't in it. After a few weak yanks, she said, "Thaddeus is right down the hall," and left. The next thing I knew in walked Thaddeus, the school janitor. And as soon as I saw his eyes—old, with a worried look in them—the fight went right out of me. So when he said, "Honey, I think you best get up and come into the hall with me," I did. That's the way Mama Cope raised me. I mean there wasn't any point in bringing trouble to old Thaddeus.

When I got home Mama Cope never did say much about the whole thing, being it wasn't my fault. But the following September she put me in St. Peter and Paul School and decided to make me Catholic.

"Betsy . . ."

For one second I imagined that Mama Cope was calling me, but the next second I knew better.

"Can I carry your suitcase?" My mother tapped my arm to get my attention.

Don't touch me. That's what I wanted to say. But Mama Cope said if you can't say something nice, don't say anything. Besides, I could tell by my mother's voice that she was trying hard to make things comfortable between us. Nonetheless, the last thing I felt like doing was handing over my suitcase with my things inside to anybody.

I dropped my eyes and stepped next to a long, brown sofa. A gold blanket covered the back and two gold towels covered the arms, almost the same shade as the blanket. I didn't notice the rest of the room because Sissy Jupe's claws were digging in Mama Cope's tulips and my chest was hurting something awful. I straddled my suitcase and steadied myself against the sofa.

"It's okay," I said, loosening his claws. "I got you."

I could feel my mother's eyes on me as I spoke, but she didn't say anything and I was glad. Not just because of her annoying questions, either. I just don't like a lot of talking. Rita Rosini says it's because I'm stubborn. But the real reason is I've learned that most people will talk until the sun goes down, if you let them. It sounds mean, but it's the truth.

I was about to lift up my suitcase when I heard laughter

and turned to see what was going on. That's when I noticed a giant bulge in the screen door. It was about the size and shape of a grown watermelon, long on the sides and fat in the middle. The picture stuck in my head, too, the same way riding in Woody's garbage truck and seeing Rita Rosini's station wagon did. Some things do that to you. They don't mean much of anything at the time, but later you can be walking down the street or drinking a soda and, for no good reason at all, your brain starts working on you and before you can blink your eyes, you have a knot in your stomach the size of a bowling ball, and the thing you thought you forgot is back and running through your head like an old 3-D movie.

My eyes gradually made their way through the screen to the porch. My father was the first one they found. He was talking to Boy Boy. Boy Boy was built like a bulldog with a big head and no neck to speak of and tiny, dumb-looking eyes that were shaped like two flattened olives. My father leaned in and Boy Boy's shoulders started moving up and down the way shoulders do when somebody's having a good laugh. I could see Mrs. Hicks, too, standing as straight as a flagpole, with her long, bony hands on her hips and her eyes, as hard as walnuts, fixed on Boy Boy's face. Boy Boy's shoulders kept moving up and down and every once in a while he would nudge my father and my father would pull out a laugh or two of his own. They sounded phony, though.

"Good to have you home," I heard my mother say.

I was about to turn back around when, out of the corner of my eye, I saw Carole and Bootsie. They were standing in front of Mrs. Hicks. I couldn't make out what they were saying because of all the laughing. I did notice that Carole was frowning.

"This way honey," my mother said, and I turned back around.

Sissy Jupe was trying to get down. I cradled him in one arm and rested my suitcase on my knee to get a tighter grip. And, at that very moment, as suddenly as it started, the laughter dried-up and everything got quiet. I didn't move because I was afraid the screen door might open and somebody might say something to me and I might be expected to say something back and I didn't have a single word for any of them.

"Are you okay?" My mother's voice sounded about as tired as I ever heard a voice sound.

I didn't know what to say. But it didn't matter. I had a feeling my mother wasn't expecting an answer. And, as if to confirm that fact, she shined her eyes on me and held them there with a sigh.

"Long day." That's what she said but her eyes told me she wanted to say something different. I understood. We were like two silent movie stars, who had to watch every word because we didn't know how it would be read later on.

"How was Woody?"

"Fine," I said, without emotion.

My mother nodded a quick nervous nod that told me she was sorry I had to ride home in a smelly garbage truck.

Sissy Jupe was clawing to get down.

"It's okay, baby," I said, and changed arms.

"Let me help." The next thing I knew my mother was holding my suitcase and opening a door that led to a small landing and fourteen of the skinniest steps you can imagine. I counted them, myself. When we got to the top, she stepped into the hallway and turned around.

"You and Bootsie'll share a bedroom," she said, patting

Sissy Jupe's head. "Carole sleeps downstairs for now."

The last part sort of caught me off balance and I wasn't sure where I was supposed to go with it. I guess my mother read confusion on my face because she continued right where she had left off.

"Not enough space," she said, with a wave of her hand.

Everything felt odd, as if my mother was talking to me and talking past me at the same time. I put my hands over my eyes and squeezed out the light. For a brief moment, I was back at Mama Cope's and Rita Rosini was there and so were our baseball cards. Two whole boxes. Rita and I were sorting them by value like we always did. I put Roger Maris on top.

"Your dress is beautiful." I opened my eyes as a light breeze blew by. It was then I noticed, for the first time, my mother smelled sweet, like a bunch of just picked flowers all mixed up in the same vase. If I'd been with Mama Cope, I would've mentioned how much I liked the smell. Instead, I pulled Sissy Jupe's claws out of my dress and stepped into the hall without answering. A moment later, we were in a small room with two small beds, two windows and no rug.

"This one is yours," my mother smiled, laying my suitcase on the bed under the window facing the street. "It's a hot one today."

I looked for a fan, but there was none.

"Get down, boy." Sissy Jupe jumped onto the bed and clawed the bedspread a few times to settle himself, then hung his paws over the side and clawed some more. I could tell by my mother's eyes that watching a new bedspread getting clawed was hard on her, but she didn't say anything. She lifted her hair to catch a light breeze. "Bootsie picked your linens," she said, tying her hair in a knot. "The pillowcases even have buttons. What will people think of next?"

I picked up the pillow. It was the color of weak tea and had shiny shell buttons along one end. The next thing I knew I was pushing my face into soft cotton and my mother was handing me a hankie.

"You don't want to dirty your new pillow." I could hear the disappointment in her voice even as she tried hard to hold onto her smile.

I put the pillow down and wiped my face on the hankie. Then I looked around. Besides the beds, which were made of metal and painted brown, there was a chair and a chest of drawers that matched the beds, except for the knobs. They were covered with red nail polish. My mother shook her head and explained how Bootsie had painted the knobs herself.

"Jean Ann, a neighbor girl, provided Bootsie the nail polish and stood there and watched." The smile my mother had worked so hard to hold onto was gone. "What did she care? It wasn't their furniture."

I didn't say anything, but I was thinking I would have used pink because pink is prettier than red.

My mother opened the top drawer. "This one and the one under it are yours. If you need more space there's a shelf in the closet."

The closet was on Bootsie's side of the room. It was about three feet wide and had a white sheet hanging down the front of it.

I must have looked puzzled because my mother said, "A few months back, your father took the door off to get up to the attic. If you need more hangers be sure to check the hall closet."

I didn't say anything, so she went on talking.

"Tomorrow, we'll call Miss Reinheart."

"To visit Mama Cope?"

"To pick up the rest of your things," my mother said, softly. "You heard the judge. No contact."

I felt my face redden with anger. What does that stupid old judge know, I wanted to scream. Instead, I bit my tongue and gathered Sissy Jupe in my arms.

My mother was standing over the second bed, smoothing the sheets for the umpteenth time. "Bootsie isn't the neatest person in the world."

I could see my mother's will coming through the pores of her face as she struggled once again to get me to respond. If she had known me at all, she would have known I wasn't one of those clever people who can say what other people want to hear. Besides, I was too tired to lie.

"Feel free to walk around and get acquainted."

"Okay," I mumbled, and sat on the bed. Moving towards the closet, my eyes spotted a hole in the wall above Bootsie's headboard. It looked as if somebody had yanked loose something and took a chunk of plaster with it. There were crayon markings on the wall, too, and pieces of Scotch Tape with brown hairs on them. I scrunched my nose, and my eyes moved along the wall until they got to the far corner. There, standing barrel side up was a baseball bat. A glove was spread over the end cap and "B-OO-T-S-IE" was written across the part where your fingers go. To make all the letters fit "O O" was on the index finger and "I E" was on the baby finger.

"Do you play baseball?"

I nodded, without checking for a reaction. I was interested in the glove, the way the leather was shaped like a real hand and had dark spots as if the glove had been worn a million times. But mostly I couldn't believe that anybody would write on a perfectly good baseball glove.

"Bootsie loves to play ball."

My mother's words were still settling in my brain when, out of the corner of my eye, I saw her reaching for my suitcase as if she were about to open it, and the next thing I remember is sitting on my suitcase, yelling, "Don't touch that it's mine."

It took me a moment to recognize the voice I was hearing was my own. My mother closed her eyes, and then opened them again.

"I didn't mean to impose. I just thought you might like a little help putting your things away."

I clutched my suitcase without answering.

"I'm sorry I haven't been able to be . . ." My mother's voice trailed off and I couldn't catch the tail end of her sentence. I thought about asking her to continue, but I could tell by her mood that she was done talking. So I carried my suitcase over to the dresser, opened the top drawer, and pushed in a pile of pants. I did the same thing with my shirts and underwear. I was about to start in on my socks when I felt a hand my shoulder.

"I should go. You and Sissy Jupe must be tired after your long trip."

I nodded.

"I'll be downstairs if you need me." My mother walked towards the door as she spoke, turning around only once when she was about to step into the hall. She was wearing a smile, only it didn't match her eyes. They looked sad.

"Thank you," I whispered, and handed her back the hankie.

"You're welcome. If you fall asleep, I'll send Bootsie up when it's time for dinner."

I didn't budge because all of a sudden I felt something sharp sticking in my leg. I turned and lifted the hem of my dress. There it was. An open safety pin with a red ribbon. Rita Rosini gave it to me to keep away the *mala occhi.* She said the evil eye didn't like red. I closed the pin.

"Are you okay?" My mother sounded concerned.

"Yes." I listened as my mother's feet made their way downstairs and the door to the dining room opened and then closed.

"Hold me, please hold me." I kissed Sissy Jupe, then tucked some loose threads into my pinafore and slowly cried myself to sleep.

III

Watchamacallit Isn't a Word

"Dinner time!" A voice went through my head like a shot. I opened my eyes. Bootsie had her hand on my arm. I swatted it like I would have swatted a pesky horsefly.

"What's wrong with you?"

I responded by running the pillow down my sweaty face.

"That's brand new. I know because I picked it out."

"Whoop-de-doo."

"You're weird."

"I know you are, what am I?"

"S-t-u-b-b-o-r-n."

The way she spelled out the word had me worried the way I always worry when people try to sound as if they know me and don't. Even so, I had a strong feeling that more was being unsaid than said and she was leaving the most important stuff out. I just didn't know what.

"You'll learn."

"Go away. I'm not hungry."

"Don't say I didn't warn you." As she spoke a feeling of panic swept through me and before I realized what was happening, I was waddling towards the dresser wrapped in a sheet.

"Give me two minutes." I pulled off my dress, dropped the sheet, and pulled on a T-shirt and shorts.

She rolled her eyes, watching. "You got ten seconds. Ten, Nine. Eight. Seven . . . ."

I took a few swipes at my hair on the way downstairs and put the comb on the windowsill at the landing. Then Bootsie opened the door and there they were seated at the table, waiting.

My mother acknowledged our presence with a smile.

"Good evening," my father said, pushing a platter of pork chops my way. "Eat up."

Carole forked a chop on its way by. "It took you two long enough to come downstairs."

"Ssshhh, not now," my mother whispered. "Give Betsy a little time to get to know us."

"You yell at me when I'm late for supper."

"Carole . . . "

My father pounded his fist on the table, "You heard your mother! Stop your goddamn whining."

I felt Bootsie nudge my leg under the table, but I didn't let on. Even so, her nudge did me a lot of good. It made me wonder if there might be more to her than I knew. Carole was a different story. She didn't seem to think too highly of either of us.

"I'm the oldest but nobody don't listen to me," she whined. "I was here first."

"*Listens*," my mother corrected. "And, *don't* is unnecessary. Pass the corn."

Carole speared both ends of a cob of corn. "I'm busy." Then she spread it with butter and raised her voice a few octaves. "They can get their own."

My mother covered her ears with her hands. "That's enough," she said.

In Carole's eyes family order meant everything. She reminded me of those twins in the Bible that hated each other because they didn't come out at the same time. Mama Cope said that one twin stole the other twin's birthright and the one that had his birthright stolen was only trying to set things straight. I told her it was hard to tell who the good brother was and who the bad brother was with all the mean stuff they kept doing to each other.

"Ouch!" Bootsie tagged my arm with a bowl of steaming home-fries.

I was tempted to elbow the bowl, but I set it down and scooped a spoonful of home-fries onto my plate. When I was done, I added a small pork chop. There was a bowl of succotash and a jar of Lucky Leaf applesauce circulating, too, but I didn't want any. When I told Bootsie I wasn't hungry, I was telling the truth. What I wanted was to be left alone. But seeing how that wasn't possible, I did what anyone would have done in the same situation; I faked an appetite. I forked a tiny piece of pork chop in my mouth and chewed until my jaws couldn't take any more chewing, then I forked an even tinier piece of potato and chewed some more.

And the whole time I was forking and chewing, I was watching my father. I could tell he didn't like me by the way his eyes stared unblinking into mine. Or it might have been that dimestore smile of his. I'm not sure. On top of all this, my brain was going backwards and forwards so fast it was hard for the rest of me to keep up. There I was chewing on home-fries wondering if Rita Rosini wanted her baseball cards back and if Mama Cope missed me as much as I missed her and if I was ever going to see them again.

A big knot formed in my throat. I had to swallow three times to get the food down. I glanced at my father. This time his eyes were glued to his plate. It was a curious sight. He was soaking up pork gravy with a slice of bread. When he was done eating the bread, he gripped the arms of his chair with both hands and parted his lips as if he were about to speak, only he didn't. Slowly, a smile came onto his face. Then he opened his mouth and sucked in air like a pitcher about to make a long throw. It was the oddest thing. It wasn't as if his plate was empty because it wasn't. The only thing missing was the gravy. He hadn't even touched his home-fries. They were sitting right next to where the gravy used to be. That didn't matter though. His eyes said it all. My father knew I was watching him and he was enjoying the attention. He could've had a live pig on his plate and it wouldn't have made any difference. He was too busy holding onto his phony smile. Then, without warning, his smile left and he put down his fork.

"What's wrong, Bill? I cooked the home-fries with chopped onion just the way you like."

While my mother talked, my father's eyes floated from face to face.

Finally he said, "Guess nobody has time for grace anymore?" and the corners of his mouth turned upward as if some invisible wire were holding his mouth in place.

My mother sighed. "Who would like to say the blessing?"

"I think Betsy should." Bootsie held a napkin over her mouth to keep from laughing.

I was shaking my head, no, when I heard my mother

say, "I'd like that."

She tried to sound cheery but I could hear exhaustion hanging onto each word. I didn't have the heart to disappoint her. I cleared my throat and began, "Bless us O Lord and these thy gifts which we are about to receive from thy bounty through Christ our Lord. Amen."

Amen was still landing when Carole saw fit to protest.

"She forgot, 'in Jesus' name.'"

My mother glanced at Carole, and in a soft voice, whispered, "Betsy says grace the Catholic way."

"Who wants to teach her the right way?"

"I will Daddy," Carole offered. "God is great and God is good . . ."

I bit my tongue to stop myself from interrupting. Before this, I had never thought much about being Catholic. But the longer Carole prayed, the more I liked the idea. If my rosary hadn't been with my clothes in Miss Reinheart's office, I would've pulled it out right there and then.

"In Jesus' name. Amen."

"Thank you girls," my mother said, and blinked her eyes as if to reset the moment.

I raised my head slowly to avoid detection and glanced at my father. He was pouring my mother more tea and for the first time, I saw something warm in his cold eyes that made him appear to have two pair of eyes, one behind the other.

"Everything okay?" It was my mother's voice. She was looking right at me.

"Fine." I wiped the lie off my lips with my napkin.

I estimated the room temperature to be about one hundred degrees. Behind the table there was a window raised shoulder height and it had a screen stretched across its middle. Every once in a while a breeze came through, but mostly hot air came in. Nobody seemed to mind, which was fine with me. I reasoned that the less any of them talked, the less I had to. I did miss air-conditioning, though.

I took a drink of milk, a long one, and checked on Bootsie. She was half sitting and half standing with one hand unscrewing the applesauce jar and the other on a pork chop she held by the bone. She looked sort of funny with her mouse-colored hair pulled into a thin ponytail and her arms, lean and muscled, going in different directions. She was just about to sink her fork in the jar when I noticed a tablespoon, bowl-side down, next to the lid, and passed it to her. But instead of taking it she sank her fork into the jar.

"Bootsie use the . . ." My mother stopped mid-sentence because she was choking.

"Cough it up." My father slapped her on the back and ordered her to spit into his hand.

After four or five good slaps, my mother said she was fine and whatever had caused her to choke was gone.

Carole pointed at us. "Why don't the both of you stare or something?"

Bootsie flashed her the bird.

Carole pretended not to notice. "Daddy saved you," she said, stroking my mother's arm.

"Can we please change the subject?" My mother's voice was sharp and to the point.

My father took a big gulp of coffee, then looked over his cup at Carole.

"I never told you about the time I was guarding a German prisoner and he tried to swallow his dog tag."

"Did you ever have to kill anybody?"

"I said, 'Change the subject,'" my mother demanded. "I'd like to talk about something pleasant for a change."

"Because I was German they put me in charge."

Oh no, I didn't want to be German. They put people in ovens.

My mother looked embarrassed. "You never went to war," she said, and I had a feeling I wasn't German after all.

And with that, my father's eyes floated from face to face and once again the room went quiet. I felt as if I was in an episode of *Twilight Zone* and everyone knew the plot, except me.

When dinner was almost over, my father put a pork chop to his mouth, bit off a chunk, and said, "Cat steal your tongues?"

"Bootsie's hogging all the whatchamacallit."

My mother held Carole's wrist for a brief moment to get her attention. "Whatchamacallit isn't a word. It's called applesauce. You have a good vocabulary, use it."

Carole mumbled something about being first born, but she was talking under her breath and I couldn't catch most of it.

"Louder," Bootsie snickered. "Nobody can hear you."

My father pointed his knife at me. "I said this would happen. First day and she's already causing problems."

My mother's eyes were blazing. She took a deep breath and blew the air out slowly. "Everyone try to calm down and refocus. Carole, why don't you tell Betsy something about yourself."

"Do I have to?"

"No, but you are the oldest."

Carole drank some milk, and then proceeded.

"I'm Carole," she said, flatly. "I'm the oldest, then Bootsie, then you. You're going to be sleeping in my bed, at least it used to be mine before Mommy said you were coming. I sleep down here now." She took another drink, and then continued. "I don't know what else to say… oh, in four months I'll be a teenager."

"That was wonderful," my father said. "Now, it's Bootsie's turn."

Bootsie nudged my leg, and then explained how Carole was the first-born and how she followed nine months later and I followed ten months after that. Then she said that she and Carole used to share a bedroom upstairs but Carole wanted her own room when she heard I was coming. And, how even though she didn't get her own room, just got a piece of the dining room and a new fold-out bed, everybody was pleased with the change.

Bootsie sure could tell a story better than Carole. I was real interested in the bed she was talking about. I figured it had to be somewhere close by. I glanced over my right shoulder: nothing. Then I glanced over my left shoulder, and against the wall that backed up to the kitchen, I saw a bed that was sandwiched in half with a pink sheet sticking out its middle. I don't know why I didn't see it earlier, but I didn't.

"You forgot something." A wide grin spread across my father's face as he talked. "*Athletics.*" He laid on the word until Bootsie nodded her head in reply.

"Oh yeah," she mumbled.

"Yes," my mother corrected. "Talk like a young lady."

"What was the name of that boy you beat in the 100 last week?"

"Frankie."

"That's right. I remember now, he was visiting the Benson's. Thought he was going to outrun my Bootsie. Shucks, not even close. You into athletics, Betsy?"

"Baseball."

"Baseball?" My father repeated the word as if his saying it meant something different than my saying it. "Hang around and you might learn a thing or two."

"Athletics isn't everything." My mother looked at me as she spoke so I forced a smile, and she kept going. "Betsy won a Blue Ribbon for an essay she wrote about Delaware."

"Not much to say." My father was about to laugh, but my mother's eyes stopped him.

"When I was you girls' age every night I read with a flashlight until I couldn't keep my eyes open. I loved the classics, *Kidnapped, Huckleberry Finn, Robinson Crusoe,* all of them."

The whole time my mother was talking I was wondering what else Miss Reinheart had told them about me.

"I read *True Romance.*" Carole used her most grown-up voice.

"I asked you to stop buying that trash," my mother said. "You're the oldest. You should be setting a good example."

"I like them," Carole whined.

"I read *Huckleberry Finn,*" I whispered, hoping that only my mother heard me.

"Wonderful," she said, and looked sort of surprised and disappointed at the same time. She opened her mouth to say more, but no words came out. I wanted to tell her how I wouldn't mind reading it again, since Mama Cope had to help me the first time around, but my mouth wasn't working any better than my mother's.

"Delicious." My father wrapped a slice of bread around a small pork chop and took a bite.

RRRRRing. It was the doorbell. My mother motioned for us to remain seated. "Not at dinner. Whoever it is can wait."

"Might be money," my father said, and with his pork chop sandwich still in his hand, he stood up and walked to the door.

"Ahhhhhhh," Carole crooned.

Bootsie laughed and Carole shot her another hateful look.

I had to drink some milk to keep from laughing.

"Bootsie gave me the finger."

"How many more times do I have to tell both of you to start acting your age?" my mother said, and for a moment there was silence.

I looked around. On the same wall as the window there was a big picture of Jesus kneeling down by a rock, praying. It was a color picture and it had a lot of gold in it like a low fire that's just getting worked up. The gold lit up the sky and narrowed into one giant ray that fell on Jesus. His eyes seemed to pull in the biggest share. They were the fieriest eyes I had ever seen and I liked looking at them. After a few moments, I had a feeling somebody was watching me. I lowered my head and my mother's eyes and mine met.

"The last thing I bought before your father and I got married," she said, almost to herself.

"It's nice," I said, and she smiled.

A moment later, I heard loud footsteps and my father stepped into the room and Boy Boy Hicks was with him. My father had his arm on Boy Boy's shoulder and Boy Boy was grinning.

"We got company," my father said. "Get another plate."

Boy Boy patted his round belly and stepped closer to the table.

I glanced at Bootsie, but she was one step ahead of me. "Take my seat," she said, and lickety-split she was standing and Boy Boy was sitting.

"Eat." My father stared at my plate as he spoke. My plate was empty.

Boy Boy ignored everything around him except scraps of food on the table, which he began eating with his fingers.

I looked up to Jesus.

"If you're finished your dinner, you may be excused." My mother patted my hand and as she did, her teacup tipped. She let out a loud sigh. I watched her straighten the cup on its saucer, then stepped away from the table.

In the bedroom window, nearly hidden by the soupy gray air of late evening, was Sissy Jupe. I turned on the light. That's when I saw my circus poster. Someone had taped it above Bootsie's headboard to hide the hole I had seen earlier. I walked towards Sissy.

"My baby." I raked my fingers through his hair and looked through the window at the growing darkness outside. Across the street, I could see two beat-up cars on concrete blocks. A little farther back, I could see car seats standing straight up and next to them were giant oil barrels with steel pipes sticking out of them.

Suddenly a dog began to howl. It was a loud persistent howl that sounded close by. I pressed my face to the screen, and, for a brief moment, I thought I saw a dog under one of the cars. But when I looked harder I realized I was looking at a truck engine or something.

Not finding the dog got me upset. The next thing I knew I was pressing my tulip dress under my nose so I could smell Mama Cope's scent. I took short quick breaths to resist crying.

I carried Sissy Jupe to bed and covered us with a sheet. The sheet seemed as important as Huck Finn's raft, the one he tried to take up river, and I was glad to have it. Mama Cope said that Huck and Jim went down river, not up, but I think she was missing the point.

"Aren't you hot?" Bootsie tapped my head through the sheet.

I could feel more tears coming. I tried to swallow them, but this time there were too many.

"I put your hairbrush on the dresser. We can talk tomorrow."

I didn't say anything. I was convinced that for this family tomorrow would be as awful as today.

"Are you really Catholic?" It was a strange question and Bootsie didn't wait for my answer. "I'm Christian like Jesus."

I was tempted to explain how Catholics are Christians and Jesus was a Jew but I was convinced the whole bunch of them were as dumb as doorknobs. Besides, I was tired.

"Did a car hit him?" Bootsie was lifting Sissy Jupe's chin and staring in his eyes.

She didn't seem to care that I wasn't talking and kept going. "I got him something," she said, and dug in her pocket for pieces of pork wrapped in a napkin. "I thought he might be hungry."

I pulled the sheet off me, ashamed. I had not fed Sissy Jupe all day.

"We don't have a litter box, but when you were asleep I took him outside and he peed and pooped."

I nodded my head, grateful.

"I'll get some water." When Bootsie returned, Sissy Jupe rubbed her arm. Then he ate the pork chop and drank the water until it was all gone.

Outside the dog started to howl again, this time louder.

IV

Dancing with Blue-Footed Boobies

Brighton Avenue marked the beginning of Jackson's Hill, a three-street offshoot of Wilmington. Nobody seemed to know how the place got its nickname being that most of it is below sea level and as flat as a bed sheet. But that didn't stop some folks from guessing.

"Named for Stonewall Jackson himself," Mr. Benson, Sarah and Jean Ann's father, told me, as if further discussion was unnecessary. I did think it odd, being Delaware is in the North (most of it anyway). But, I kept quiet because when Mrs. Benson made ham and cabbage, they invited me over, and I didn't want to jinx myself by saying the wrong thing.

Later Bootsie told me that people from South Carolina are always running some confederate general's name up a flagpole and waving it in everybody's face.

"Don't listen," she said in a stern voice. "Stonewall Jackson never set foot in Delaware. Daddy said his own men killed him for being a coward."

I took a deep breath and looked around a few times, storing up patience. I wasn't sure if Stonewall Jackson ever set foot in Delaware, but I was sure his death was accidental and his men never got over it. I was also sure that Bootsie believed Yankees were better than Confederates and no amount of talking was going to change that. Her feelings seemed rooted in some sort of numerical genealogical truth my father had uncovered when he looked at the North and South. He never explained himself, but he said, "The facts are all there for anyone to see." I didn't see any of it, especially since every house in Jackson's Hill had at least one native born southerner, except us. My father was almost born in Manassas, but his mother held out until she reached Wilmington to give birth. It was one of his favorite stories. "The only sane thing she ever did her entire life," he would add, and I said (without uttering a word): If you can't say something nice, don't say anything—just like Mama Cope taught me.

With only three streets, Jackson's Hill was an easy place to miss if you didn't live there or know where you were going. Brighton Avenue was in the middle and the only street with houses clear to the end. The other two streets, Central and Exmore, were cut short by the same stretch of high grasses and high trees that formed the marshy back-end of Brighton. There, every day at noon, a train sounded a mournful whistle and Mr. Benson stood at the end of his big horseshoe driveway; and, with his right hand squared to his forehead, saluted Stonewall Jackson.

A few houses down Mrs. Samson, who replaced her dead husband, Jimmy Dean, with a pet monkey named

Coco, watched with disgust as the train passed.

"Fool whistle," she said dropping banana peels into the pocket of her apron. "Scared Coco so bad one time he ran off and the police found him five miles away hiding under a porch. There was even a write-up about him in the Sunday paper. I told that young reporter the same thing I told them train people. Coco would be a good monkey if it weren't for that God-awful whistle blowing all hours of the day and night."

Mrs. Samson complained a lot, but I was more interested in Coco than hearing about some train. He sure was cute, with big brown eyes and human-looking fingers, and a long tail with black stripes.

I wanted to introduce myself, so I walked closer and said, "Hi, I'm Betsy."

"Better watch yourself," Mrs. Samson warned. "His teeth are sharp, I wouldn't want you getting hurt."

I drew my hand back and watched Coco scratch his neck with one hand and push pieces of banana into his mouth with the other.

My monkey, I said, almost out loud, wondering if he would sit on my lap and rub my arm like a cat.

Suddenly, Mrs. Samson undid Coco's collar and his chain slithered like a long snake down the neck of the magnolia tree.

"Enough sun for one day," she said, trapping Coco in the bend of her long, fleshy arm. "Let's go inside before that whistle starts up again."

Mrs. Samson wrapped the chain loosely around her wrist as she talked. When she was done, she motioned towards the house.

"How would you like to join Coco and me for lunch?" The words had barely fallen out of her mouth, when I was imagining Coco and me sharing a bottle of 7-Up and a grilled cheese sandwich with sliced tomato. Then, just as Coco was taking a swig of 7-Up and looking at me like he wanted to be mine, a man's voice came out of nowhere, shouting my name. I tried to act deaf, but the voice wouldn't let up.

"Betsy . . . Betsy!"

"That's your father calling. You better go see what he wants."

"*Betsyyyyyyyyy.*"

"Hurry child!" Mrs. Samson's eyes were wide with fear. I sensed I should be afraid, too, so I looked towards the street, then I looked at Coco. "Good monkey," I mumbled, without moving.

"Go on, go, you can visit again."

Mrs. Samson pushed me forward, and I pulled in a mouthful of air and took off. My legs didn't stop until I reached Mrs. Hicks' lilac bush. It was in full bloom and its cone-shaped sweetness perfumed the hot, humid air. I took in a noseful and held onto it as I walked up the slate sidewalk that split our yard and her yard down the middle.

My father was on the porch, waiting. Three weeks had passed since I had arrived, and I still found it awkward to call people I barely knew, Mommy and Daddy. My father picked up on this and ordered me to say, 'Daddy' or "There will be hell to pay." This was another threat too vague for me to understand. It seemed like every time he opened his mouth, I had to try to guess what he meant. I always assumed the worst.

"Hi," I said.

"Hi, what?" He was smoking a corncob pipe that he held by the bowl.

"Hi Daddy."

"See, that wasn't so hard, was it?" He was smiling, but I wasn't sure why.

I shook my head, no.

"Where the hell you been?" The smile was gone and a frown had taken its place.

"I umm . . ."

"You forget?" He paused to spit bits of tobacco into his hand and wipe his hand on his overalls, the kind painters wear, with thick shoulder straps and a wide pocket across the chest.

"No, Daddy."

"I asked you a question," he sneered. "I've been calling you for an hour."

I knew my father was lying. I also knew I had no choice, but to play along. So I summoned up my sincerest voice and said: "I was at Coco's."

My father pulled a can of Prince Albert out of his pocket and stuffed some tobacco in the bowl of his pipe and set it on fire. Then, he took a long draw and blew the smoke out slowly. "So, what you're saying is you prefer being with a goddamn monkey more than your own family."

"No," I said, stepping onto the porch.

The next thing I remember is his hand pushing against my chest and my feet rising up, and having a terrible sensation I was falling backwards and there was nothing I could do to save myself. Then, suddenly, out of the corner of my eye, I saw the stair railing and my fingers groped for it until a large splinter punctured my thumb, and I pulled back. Then just when I was sure that I was a goner, I felt a hand grab my arm and stop my fall.

"You trying to hurt yourself?" My father spoke softly, but his voice was cold.

"No, Daddy," I said, squeezing the splinter free.

"Didn't that Cope woman teach you anything?"

"Yes."

"Yes, what?"

"Yes, Daddy."

My father laughed until his voice dried up. Then he cleared his throat and laughed some more. Finally, he poked the stem of his pipe into my cheek. "You'll learn," he said. "Sooner or later."

I could feel my skin redden with anger.

"You pushed me." The words fell out of my mouth quickly the way the truth does when you aren't expecting it.

He poked the pipe into my cheek, this time harder.

I tried to back up, but he stopped me. "Mama Cope isn't here, I am." It was a mean thing to say and it hit its mark.

"That chapter of your life is over," he said, and crushed his body into mine. "I'm in charge now." Sweat dripped off of his chin onto my neck. I turned my head to breathe, and he responded by pressing my face into his chest. His body smelled of paint and tobacco. I tried to break free, but he was too strong. My hand was throbbing.

My father's eyes went up and down my face. "You look a lot like your mother did when we met."

The words would have sounded nice if he hadn't said them in a way that sent chills down my spine. I tried to turn my head, but he had hold of my chin. He took a puff on his pipe and blew out the smoke. The smoke made the air turn to fog and my eyes burn.

"You'll learn ... Bug... s."

Once again I felt completely clueless. Was he calling me a bug? No, Bugs. He emphasized the "s" like Bugs Bunny. I began to wonder if something was wrong with me. Something I didn't know about. Something that made him hate me. I couldn't come up with anything, though, except for looking like my mother.

"Daddy's just testing you." Bootsie was always trying to make me feel better by coming up with some strange explanation for his behavior. But, when I asked why I was being tested, she shrugged, "To watch your reaction."

"Like Pavlov's dog?"

Bootsie didn't answer, so I tried another direction.

"How come he doesn't test *you*? He likes you."

Bootsie rolled her eyes. But it was the truth. She was his favorite because she was stronger and quicker than most boys and this pleased my father greatly. One Saturday he gathered up the neighborhood bullies for what he called the Brighton Avenue Track Events and offered a quarter to anyone who could outrun her. Of course, nobody could. So this left Bootsie holding a fistful of quarters. The next day Bootsie and I were on our way to Tull's Drugstore to buy Cokes and candy with the winnings when Butchie Boswell showed up. It was obvious from the look on his face he was up to no good. He followed us all the way to Tull's and waited until we were inside to make his move. Bootsie was chewing on a Three Musketeer bar when he stepped in front of her, eyeball to eyeball, and said: "Let's see what a big shot you are without your father around."

I could see the muscles in Bootsie's face go tense, but she didn't bat an eyelash.

"Get lost, jerk," she said, and took another chew. Well, I guess that was too much for Butchie because he hauled off and punched her in the side. The Three Musketeer flew out of her hand and she tried like crazy to catch it. She almost had it, too, but her arm hit the gumball machine. The next thing we knew about a million gumballs and all sorts of shiny prizes were pouring out all over the floor. Mr. Tull stood right there and never said a word.

Butchie raised his fist again, but this time Bootsie was ready for him. She backed up a degree or two, and with one quick move, landed a right to his eye. Butchie let out a loud moan, then cupped his face in his hands, and ran out of the door, cursing. That's when Mr. Tull looked at the floor and said, "No good to me now. You girls help yourselves." Well, Bootsie and I worked like demons, scooping up whistles and balls and rings with rubies and diamonds in them. When every prize was safely in our pockets, we went for the gum. After we were done we had to walk like we had two wooden legs and no knees to keep from losing everything. And it didn't help to hear Mr. Tull laughing. But we finally made it home without losing a single gumball.

"Let's sell the gum to Sarah and Jean Ann," Bootsie said, so we did. Of course, we didn't pass on any of the particulars about how we got our loot, so everything went real smooth. Sarah and Jean Ann paid fifty-eight cents for fifty-five gumballs. Bootsie explained the extra three cents covered shipping and handling. After the sale, she got a Kinney shoebox and wrote WAMPUM on top and put the money inside. Then she put her track winnings in and said, "This is both of ours, okay?" I gave my word.

The next day we were riding bikes and we saw Butchie down by the creek, fishing. He was wearing the biggest shiner I ever saw. Later that same day my father saw it for himself and paid Bootsie an extra dollar.

"You earned this," he said, counting out quarters in her hand. "Boy, am I proud."

When my father left, I asked Bootsie, "Why does he want you to be a boy?"

I saw her eyes catch my question. But she sure took

a long time to answer. I was starting to walk away when I heard her voice coming up behind me. "I don't know," she said. "Just does, that's all."

Later that day I was on the porch when she pulled me inside. "C'mon, we need to look busy. Daddy'll be home any second."

I was pouring Kool-Aid in cold water and Bootsie was dropping in ice cubes, when my father walked in and circled the room with his eyes.

"What are you two up to?" he growled, but my mother was in no mood to hear him.

"Don't start," she said, and threw a wet dishrag at him to make her point.

"You haven't seen anything yet," he said, and left.

Bootsie and I each drank a glass of Kool-Aid. Afterward, my mother reminded us to take Sissy Jupe outside. "Pay attention. Remember, he depends on you to be his eyes."

After Sissy Jupe was done peeing in Mrs. Hicks' newly planted tomato garden, Bootsie and I walked around front trying to decide if Sitting Bull or Chief Joseph was the best Indian ever born. Of course, I was in Chief Joseph's camp.

"Sitting Bull was braver," Bootsie countered.

"Wrong." I barely got the word out when I smelled lit tobacco and felt something heavy hit my back. It was a gallon of Dutch Boy paint. My father had swung it just hard enough to push me forward, but not so hard that I let go of Sissy Jupe or fell head first on the ground.

"You may fool some people," he said. "But you don't fool me ... not for a second."

Bootsie reached for the can of paint. "Put this in Daddy's car and I'll watch Sissy," she said, taking Sissy Jupe from me and setting him on the ground.

I was closing the car door when my father grabbed the

handle and growled. "Careful."

"Yes, Daddy." There was no mistaking his message: I was the black sheep of the family and he intended to do everything in his power to make sure I understood this point.

As his car pulled away, black smoke from under the hood shadowed it up the street.

"The engine's . . ." Before Bootsie had a chance to finish her thought Mrs. Hicks was pulling her new Olds 98 up to the curb. I looked over just in time to see her lift something heavy off the front seat.

"These here are for my Boy Boy," she said, carrying an armload of records towards the house. "Sweet Jesus music."

I didn't say anything, but I couldn't help thinking that Boy Boy liked beer and girls a whole lot more than he liked Jesus. I remembered the evening I was looking out the window and I saw him drinking beer and trying to put his hand down some girl's blouse. She kept trying to get away, but he had her pinned against a cement clothes pole pretty good. Finally, the girl let him have a feel. But, after that she called him a pig and said she never wanted to see him again. I didn't catch the rest because it got dark and everything got real quiet once she stopped talking.

Anyway, all of a sudden Mrs. Hicks let out a loud sneeze and the next thing I knew, Sissy Jupe was jumping off my lap and records were flying everywhere.

"Ohhhhh my Lord." Mrs. Hicks dropped to her knees and raked records into a pile. "Get that *thing* away from me."

I asked Bootsie to take Sissy Jupe inside and I offered to help.

"At least one of you girls has manners," Mrs. Hicks

said, and I noticed that her false teeth made small sucking sounds whenever she tried to smile and talk at the same time.

"This here's my favorite." She was holding up an album cover with a smiling Jesus and a baby lamb on the cover.

I nodded, politely.

"I lent these to a friend at church," she said, handing me a pile of records. "But I sure did miss my music."

I made my way up the steps, onto the porch.

"This way," she said, motioning me inside. "Wipe your feet."

I slid my feet on a coir mat and sat the records on a long red and tan sofa covered in shiny plastic. Across from the sofa was a red chair dressed the same way. There was more plastic on the floor. It was cut in long strips and went from the front door to the sofa and over to the chair and out to the dining room. Under the plastic was thick tan carpet that looked brand new. Besides the sofa and chair, the only other piece of furniture in the room was a small television with a ceramic clock on top painted to resemble Jesus.

I was staring at the clock when I heard Mrs. Hicks' teeth making sucking sounds again, only this time louder. I turned around just in time to see her top teeth tilt away from her gum and her tongue tease them back in place. I closed my eyes in case her teeth were planning to escape. When the sucking sounds stopped I opened my eyes.

"You think you might enjoy coming to church with me sometime?"

"I'm Catholic." The words fell out of my mouth automatically.

"Oh, we aren't prejudice. We welcome anybody."

"Thanks," I blurted out, and stepped onto the porch

and breathed in some fresh air.

Moments later I heard what sounded like a record player cranking up followed by a loud, high-pitched scream.

I plugged my ears with my fingers and waited for the racket to ease up. But the screaming got louder. "Rock of Ages cleft for me ..." Gradually, I could make out Mrs. Hicks' voice. It all but drowned out the voice on the record. "Let me hide myself in Thee ...."

I went inside. Bootsie was in the kitchen eating Hershey's chocolate by the tablespoon.

"He walks with me and He talks to me and ..." Mrs. Hicks was starting a new song and the voice on the record was still on the previous one.

Bootsie folded her ear towards me and yelled, "Holy Roller."

"What?"

Bootsie slid the spoon back in the can of chocolate, then scraped the spoon clean with her teeth.

"Disgusting ... nobody wants your germs."

"Who says they don't?" she said, smartly.

I ignored her dumb question because I had a question of my own.

"What's a Holy Roller?"

I could tell by the grin on her face that me not knowing something was doing her a lot of good. She waved the spoon in my face and said, "You don't know?"

I decided to negotiate. "Tell me and I'll tell you about Blue-footed Boobies."

She dropped the spoon in the sink. "It better be good."

"It is ... when the male bird likes a female bird, he dances and she rates him just like they do on Bandstand."

"Galapagos."

I was impressed and surprised. "If you knew, why didn't

you just say so?"

"Because I expected you to underestimate me, you always do." I let her remark pass with a smile because I wanted to move on. "Okay, what's a Holy Roller?"

"In church they roll themselves on the floor... that's how they got their name."

"Really?"

"Yep, I went to church once with Mrs. Hicks and I saw the whole thing. At first the preacher sounded Baptist. Then an old man stood up and hollered, 'Amen Lord' at the top of his lungs and fell to the floor and rolled around, as if he had swallowed some bad sausage for breakfast. A younger woman stood over him and I thought she might be his daughter by the way she was crying and moaning. Only, she didn't lift a finger to help. No, she fell to the floor, too, and pretty soon everybody was falling to the floor and kicking and hollering something awful."

I was excited to hear more. "Where was Mrs. Hicks?"

"She went down right after the old man and the woman."

"Was Woody there?"

"He doesn't go to church. He works a lot. That's how she got that new car. You know my baseball glove with my name on it?"

Bootsie had a way of changing the subject mid-stream, but this time I didn't mind. "Yes," I said, eager to hear more.

"Woody gave it to me and he gave me a wallet with a dollar in it."

"How come?"

Bootsie shrugged. "He thinks a hobo off one of the trains dropped it. One night one knocked on our door and Mommy gave him a bologna and cheese sandwich and chips."

"A real hobo with a stick on his shoulder and a ball of clothes on it?"

"Nope, he took the sandwich, tipped his hat, and said, 'Thank you, Ma'am,' and left."

I was disappointed to hear how plain sounding hobos are, so I mumbled a few words for the sake of politeness, then changed the subject.

"Raining," I said, walking over to the window. The window had a metal awning that was bent on one side. As drops of rain fell onto the awning, they ricocheted and made a soft, soothing sound on the window like the ticking of an old clock.

"I miss my foster parents and brother and sister."

I could hardly believe my ears.

"You had a foster family? How long?"

"Until last year."

"Were they nice?"

"Every night I dream there's a knock on the door and a paper says they're my real family, and they take me home."

"Do you get to see them?"

She shook her head, no.

"Did Carole live with foster parents?"

"She weighed two pounds when she was born, so Mommy said they had to keep her."

Finally, I understood why Carole made such a big deal over being first. She must have gotten used to being an only child. Then, years later, we showed up and she got confused.

At that moment, other things began to make sense, too. "Why does he want you to be a boy?" My words came back to me along with Bootsie's response. "Just does, that's all." There was something odd about the way my father expected people to act the way he wanted them to, or else, "There will be hell to pay."

"I was wondering," Bootsie said. "How did you get the name Betsy?"

"How did you get the name Bootsie?"

"I asked you first."

"So?"

"Just answer me."

I could tell by her mood it was best to give in, so I said, "Mama Cope. Betsy is a nickname for Elizabeth."

Bootsie smiled. "Mom Horner nicknamed me Bootsie because I had tiny feet and wore booties."

Suddenly, the sky got dark. As bolts of lightning sliced through the summer sky, I decided to play "make believe." Mama Cope taught me the game to get my mind off of where I am when I want to be someplace else. I wanted to be in the Galapagos. And a moment later there I was, like pure magic, with Blue-footed Boobies, and God was putting on a gigantic fireworks show just for me.

"Want to play cards?" Bootsie said.

"Not now," I said. "I'm dancing."

V

Caesar Rodney Isn't Going Anywhere

A few days later Carole was in the doorway of the dining room, with one hand on her hip and the other pointed at Bootsie and me.

"What are you two whispering about?" she said.

"For me to know and for you to find out." Bootsie had one hand on her hip and the other pointed at Carole.

"Mommy, they're copying me. . . ." Before Carole could finish her sentence, my mother appeared. She was wearing her hair in a French twist and a frown on her face.

"You girls should be ashamed of yourselves for acting like five-year-olds."

"They started it."

My mother sighed. "Carole, if I need anyone's two cents I'll ask for it."

Bootsie let out a breath of satisfaction and followed it

up with an angelic, "Mommy, you look pretty."

My mother tucked a piece of loose hair behind her ear, and held it in place with a bobby pin. "Thank you," she said sweetly. "You get more flies with honey than with vinegar."

Carole's eyes were burning with revenge. But my mother's words held them in check.

"I don't want nothing to do with them," Carole mumbled.

"I don't want *anything*," my mother corrected. "How many times do I have to tell you that two negatives don't make a positive?"

"Fine, I don't never want anything to do with them."

My mother glared at Carole, then walked over to the rain-soaked window and looked out. "Let's go to the library. At least there you can't fight."

Bootsie lowered her eyes to half-mast and pressed the palm of her hand to her forehead. "I don't feel good," she swooned, as if she were about to pass out.

"You don't feel *well*," my mother corrected. "It's just as easy to say something correctly as incorrectly."

"Check my forehead."

Replacing Bootsie's hand with her own, my mother's eyes, which were full of suspicion, softened. "My, you are hot . . . ."

Carole regarded Bootsie with an icy stare. "I bet she's faking."

My mother shook her head. "Bootsie get upstairs. And Carole I'm fed up with your shenanigans."

"I didn't do nothing."

"Anything." She was talking to Carole but my mother's face was pressed against the window, causing beads of wetness to scatter beneath her warm skin, then regroup and run down the cool glass.

"I want to take ballet lessons," Carole said.

My mother turned around and dried her face on the sleeve of her dress.

"Where did ballet come from all of a sudden?" she said. "We can't even pay the bills we have."

Our family lived week to week. One week we had the phone and the next week we didn't. Electricity was the same as the phone. So was the newspaper. Mr. Coen, the bread man, was the nicest. He sold on credit right up until my father bought pockets full of Irish Sweepstakes tickets and our bill went unpaid for weeks. Then there would be a note on the door and my mother's eyes would get red and she and my father would get into a yelling match. He would say she was too emotional to understand the physics of winning and she would say only a fool throws money in the air and expects more to come down than went up.

At their loudest, I worried that Mrs. Hicks would call the police and our yard would be full of black and whites. The police never came, though, and the following day my mother would short-change the landlord and bread would appear on our porch and the phone and lights would be back on.

"Bootsie always gets to do what she wants. I don't see why I can't."

"Which library?" I said it to shut Carole up.

My mother's eyes brightened considerably. "In town across from the post office."

I didn't know where the post office was. But I knew that my library, the one Mama Cope took me to, wasn't across from it. I guess I looked disappointed because my mother said, "Have you ever been there?" She used the kind of voice people use when they ask a question, but aren't real sure if they want an answer.

"No, but I'll go."

"Have fun," Carole stuck her tongue out at me, and then stomped upstairs.

It took my mother and me twenty-five minutes and two buses to get to the library. I was wearing a pair of Bootsie's blue jeans and a T-shirt. Most of my clothes were still at Miss Reinhold's, and the more my mother asked about getting them, the more my father resisted. My mother would push on, but he always had to have the final word: No.

The driver of the second bus only had one leg and one hand. He was short, too, and had to sit on three pillows in order to see out the window and line his hand up with the steering wheel. He drove all right, though. I watched him the whole way.

"You don't see the driver whining," my mother said, after stepping safely off of the bus onto the curb. "The Lord helps those who help themselves."

The driver waved his handless arm at us, and pulled away. My mother offered me the umbrella. Since she was only a little taller than I was I took it. I didn't even need to stretch. The rain had slowed considerably, but the wind was blowing and, as we walked, we got wet.

"There it is." My mother was pointing to a big, stone building. Around the outside were carvings of winged creatures with heads like men and bodies like lions. The main entrance had huge double doors that were about fifty-feet tall and somebody had carved pictures on them. Above the doors was written: "1788 Wilmington Public Library 1922."

"When I was your age my mother and I came every Saturday, rain or shine. Read and keep an open mind. That's what she always said. She was Quaker . . . ."

Since William Penn and Benjamin Franklin were Quakers I wanted to ask if they were related to us, but I wasn't sure if the question was on some sort of do-not-ask list.

"Beautiful, isn't it?"

As I nodded, it suddenly occurred to me I might have seen the library the day Mama Cope and I went to see the judge. However, I knew I never saw the front, because if I had, it would've stuck in my mind. Not because of the carving, but because the front of the library faces the backside of a bronze horse carrying Caesar Rodney up Market Street. Only Caesar Rodney isn't going anywhere because he's on a metal horse and he was dead before he was put up there. The whole thing's just there to let people know what Caesar Rodney would've looked like if he wasn't already dead.

It started to rain harder. I studied the carved pictures and my mother never rushed me.

"See under the dates?" she said, drawing closer.

"There's a laurel wreath circling two hands holding a flaming torch. Do you know what they symbolize?"

I didn't.

"The hands and torch symbolize our need for knowledge and the laurel wreath symbolizes wisdom. Without books we might just as soon be living back in the jungle."

I liked how she thought, but this time I didn't agree, not one hundred percent anyway. She was implying that books make people smart and civilized. There's a lot of good learning in books. On the other hand, Indians didn't have books and they got along just fine until white men came and herded whole tribes into the desert to teach them how to farm and pray like white folks. Mama Cope read me all about it once.

But, I was in no mood to talk. The rain was blowing right at us so my mother pointed the umbrella and me towards the door.

"How many books am I allowed?"

"As many as you can read. The more you read, the better."

Once inside, we walked up and down narrow aisles and my mother pointed out which books had "character." In her opinion, character was everything because it offered *substance*.

"Here." She pulled a book off a shelf and handed it to me. "*The Boxcar Children* is a wonderful story about four orphans who live in an abandoned boxcar rather than be separated."

I was already holding *Little Women* and *Kidnapped*, so I took the book and eased my way to the checkout counter before she had a chance to find a few more books loaded with character.

Outside, the rain was coming down harder. No matter how I turned the umbrella, rain sprayed me in the face. I was almost regretting the trip, when my mother nudged me towards Woolworth's Five and Dime. The store was square like the library and almost as big. But it was made out of brick, not stone, and had giant windows with books and buckets and blankets and blocks in them.

"Let's go in and get a bite to eat. I can use a cup of hot tea."

I didn't say anything, but my feet kept moving. There was an awning above the door and under the awning was a man with no legs on a crate with wheels. "Good to see you, Stanley," my mother smiled, and dropped two quarters in a tin cup.

"You, too," the man said, and I noticed his arms were muscled like a soldier's arms. I wondered if he had lost his legs in the war and he was finally home and still legless.

As we stepped inside, I closed the umbrella and looked

around. Along the left wall there was a lunch counter and it seemed to go on for miles and every three or four feet there were pink, blue, and white bouquets made out of balloons. The balloons were small and round and tied to the counter with pink or blue ribbons.

"What are they for?" I said, pointing to the nearest bouquet.

"Banana splits," my mother said. "You pick a balloon and inside the balloon is a piece of paper with a price on it. One time I was sitting next to a man who got a banana split for a penny."

"What's the highest price?"

"One dollar."

"Can I try?"

"Sure, but you have to eat something nutritious first."

I looked over the menu and ordered a cup of chicken soup because I could eat it fast and get to the balloons.

"Are you sure that's all you want?" My mother's eyes had big question marks in them.

"Can I get a bowl?" I noticed the cost was only twenty cents more.

"Of course, you'll have plenty of room for dessert."

I ate my soup and my mother kept pushing her grilled cheese at me until I finally convinced her my soup was plenty filling. I was glad I did, too, because she seemed to enjoy that grilled cheese, immensely. When she wasn't looking, I watched her mop warm cheese off of her plate with her bread and catch stray crumbs on the return trip.

Anyway when we were done eating, my mother signaled the waitress. The waitress was tall and thin and wore a white uniform with a gold pin across one pocket that read: "Patsy." When she walked towards us, she kept her chin up and her eyes focused just above our heads.

"Anything else?" she said, without lowering her eyes. I had never seen a waitress act so rude. I gave her a dirty look.

My mother pointed to the balloons. "My daughter would like to pick one," she said, taking a sip of tea.

"Go ahead," the waitress said, without feeling.

I reached across the counter for a pink balloon. I even smiled. The waitress popped it with her fingernail and a tiny piece of folded paper fell into my empty bowl.

I wiped the paper clean with my napkin. Be a penny, be a penny, I kept saying over and over in my head.

The waitress folded her arms across the front of her uniform. Behind her, I caught a glimpse of myself in the mirror. I looked poor. I knew this was how the waitress saw me, too. For a brief moment, I wanted to throw the piece of paper at the mirror and scream, "You don't know me, Miss Patsy whoever you think you are."

I would have done it, too, but my mother stopped me.

"Go ahead," she whispered, "read what it says."

I ironed the paper flat with the tips of my fingers. Then I read: "Eighty cents."

I closed my eyes, quickly, then opened them again: "Eighty cents."

I threw the paper on the counter. I was robbed. I was supposed to get the paper with a penny on it.

"Don't act that way." My mother handed the paper to the waitress. "You did fine. We saved twenty cents." As she spoke, I saw the disappointment in her eyes and I looked away, ashamed.

"Twenty cents," I repeated. But inside I was thinking that my mother was the sort of person who looks for rainbows anywhere. This sudden realization struck me as sad, but I didn't yet know why.

Anyway, my mother and I shared the banana split, and when our spoons scooped up the same piece of banana, we laughed and I almost forgot about picking the wrong balloon and getting robbed.

When we were done, she reached in her handbag and took out three dollars and handed them to the waitress. "Keep the change," she smiled. The waitress walked away without responding.

"Rude," I said, out loud.

"Sssshhhh." My mother tucked the umbrella under one arm and put the other around my waist. "Two wrongs don't make a right... follow me."

We took the escalator downstairs. I didn't say anything because I suspected that she was planning some special surprise.

The escalator emptied into a big windowless basement. There were signs hanging from the ceiling announcing the location of various departments. On the left of the escalator were long racks full of clothing patterns and giant rolls of cloth. On the right was the toy department. I checked out the Hula Hoops and Silly Putty and popguns and lassos made out of red, white and blue paper glued to a stick. My mother didn't rush me. I didn't ask for anything because I had a Hula Hoop, Silly Putty and a popgun at Miss Reinhold's. I did want a lasso, but decided to store that request for later.

"Ready?"

I nodded, yes, and let my mother go ahead in case she was thinking about holding my hand or doing something else I wasn't ready for.

At the end of the toy department was the fish department. Here, glass tanks were full of fish, turtles, and lizards. The lizards were the best. I watched one eat a cricket. He was as quick as lightning. And, once he had the cricket in his mouth he kept chomping and chomping until he finally got the back legs in and all. Boy, I wanted that lizard. I reasoned I could feed him crickets from Mrs. Benson's garden and he would be happy.

"Can I buy him?" I was pointing to the lizard with the cricket.

I guess that wasn't the time to ask because my mother covered her eyes and said: "Oh Lord, he's eating the legs." Then she started towards the opposite wall, and I realized I wasn't going to get a lizard no matter how badly I wanted one.

"There's enough suffering in this world," she said. "We don't need to bring it home with us."

When we got to where they sold wallpaper, my mother picked up a thick envelope with a picture of the moon and stars on it.

"Just what I was looking for," she said, holding the envelope up to the light. Inside were paper cutouts of the moon and stars. "They glow in the dark like the real ones."

"Ohhhhhhh," I said, trying to sound interested.

"Reminds me of Heaven."

I never heard my mother talk about Heaven, so I decided to take a chance and ask her about something that had been bothering me.

"Do you go to church?"

My mother dropped her eyes as if she were about to apologize for something.

"Do you miss it?"

I had to think for a minute about that one. I liked church fine most of the time, but I didn't like early Mass because Father Simms sounded like he was mostly asleep and there was no singing.

"I like singing."

"Baptists sing." My mother gave the cashier a dollar and put the moon and the stars in a paper bag.

"I thought you said you were Quaker."

"I was growing up, but your father grew up Baptist."

Outside, the rain had finally stopped and the sun was starting to climb out from behind the clouds. We stood at the bus stop and neither of us said anything for the longest time. I thought about the driver with one leg and one hand, hoping we would see him again. Finally, a bus pulled up and we stepped inside. "Would you like it if we went to church this Sunday?" my mother said over her shoulder.

I glanced past her to the driver. He had two hands and two legs.

"I guess so," I said, disappointed.

On the ride home I got to questioning myself about whether my mother was Quaker or Baptist. I finally decided she was Baptist. Her comment about my father is what settled it for me.

That night after the dinner dishes were done, Bootsie and I went to Woody's lot to play baseball (and be away from my father). After she hit six homers I threw my first slider, and when it connected with the sweet spot on her bat I knew it would take us twenty minutes to find the ball, and it did. By then, it was getting dark, so we went inside.

"Upstairs," my mother said, excitedly, and there, stuck to our ceiling, were the fake moon and stars.

"Wow . . . great!" I didn't expect Bootsie to make a fuss over a fake moon and stars, but I could tell by her voice she was sincere. Even after my mother left, she kept talking about how real they looked. "Now we can pretend we live outside like the Indians did."

"Indians lived in teepees and longhouses."

"*And outside*. C'mon, let's play. You can be Chief Joseph."

I shook my head, no, and I began reading *The Boxcar Children*.

My mother looked in at us. "Turn off the light," she said, pressing her finger to her lips.

"One more minute?"

"No." She reached for the light switch and the moon and the stars glowed down at us.

A moment later I felt my mother's soft lips on my cheek. Then she kissed Bootsie.

"Sleep tight," she said. "Tomorrow is a whole new day."

VI

On Stage

The next Sunday I put on my tulip dress, the one with the pinafore. But the buttons pulled when I tried to fasten them. I never liked the dress, but seeing how I was never going to wear it again seemed to change all that. All of a sudden, I realized that if we didn't pick up my clothes soon, nothing would fit. I felt a giant headache coming on.

"Try this." Bootsie was holding up a raggedy red dress with a plastic belt.

I reached without looking because I was trying to convince myself the dress was only sort of ugly: not *totally* ugly.

"Forget it." Bootsie threw the dress on the floor. "I don't give a shit."

"Don't cuss."

"Sorry, I forgot you're special."

"You said it, I didn't." I was proud of myself for using her own words to make my point. Still, it didn't feel quite right because she did mean well, so I put the dress on and buckled my pink shoes. I looked poor.

My mother glanced in at us. "Hurry girls, after church we're going to . . ."

"Miss Reinheart's?" I spoke quickly before my mother could say, no.

"When I say so," she said, parroting my father.

I was fuming. Most of me hated the way she avoided confrontation by reducing everything to as few words as possible. But, another part wanted to preserve – even admired – the glint she would get in her eye when she knew she had successfully achieved her goal.

"Two minutes," she said, and left.

I pinned Rita Rosini's red ribbon under my hem. I didn't really believe it had magic powers, but I could use all the help I could get.

"All set." I flattened a handkerchief across my head and bobby-pinned it in place.

Bootsie stared at my hair, but she didn't say anything.

Downstairs the whole family was waiting. We all piled in the car and headed for church. Only my father never got out when the rest of us did.

"Bill," my mother whispered, so passers-by couldn't hear. "You're not setting a good example." Then she closed the door and my father drove off.

The church was in a converted movie house and it had those seats that fold up when you're not sitting in them. The back of the seats was metal and somebody had written "hell" and "shit" and telephone numbers all over them. Somebody else had tried to cover it up with green paint, but it didn't do any good because the letters were cut deep and showed through. On stage behind where the minister stood, a big wood cross was hung in front of where a movie screen used to be. Somebody forgot to put Jesus on the cross, but Bootsie said they did it on purpose.

"Baptists aren't supposed to think about Him dying just how nice He was to people."

I was about to explain why Catholics make a habit of remembering Jesus' death when the minister started yelling something about the devil dressing up in a top hat and collecting dark souls and I don't know what else. I kept waiting for him to read from the Bible to explain himself, but he never did. He just kept waving it side to side above his head, yelling. When he was done, he kissed the Bible and everybody went wild clapping and shouting, "Amen, Jesus. Amen! Praise the Lord." The minister let them go on a while, and then he said, "Yes, the Devil tempted Jesus. He took him on top of the highest mountain and said, 'Look around, Jesus. Follow me and everything you see–all the kingdoms of the world–will be yours.'"

The minister was working up a good sweat, so he mopped his forehead with a handkerchief. For a whole minute he didn't say a word and everyone remained quiet. Then the minister stuffed the handkerchief in his pocket and his voice came back louder than ever. "What did Jesus tell the Devil?" he shouted. "He said, 'Get away from me Satan.'"

The minister kissed the Bible again. In a slow voice he said, "What are you going to tell Satan when he comes for you?"

His eyes went around the room twice and finally settled on my head. Suddenly, all eyes were on me.

"Get away Satan," somebody in the back yelled.

"Only those who remain faithful are safe," the minister boomed. "For it is written that man shall worship the Lord thy God and only He shalt thou serve."

There were more "Amens" and then everybody stood up and raised their hands over their heads, clapping. The minister let them go on awhile before he started up the choir by nodding in their direction.

"Rock of Ages cleft for me, let me hide myself in thee . . . ." The singing sounded all right but I couldn't get into it because it was the same songs that Mrs. Hicks hollered all the time.

My mother tapped my shoulder to stop my eyes from roving. I unpinned the handkerchief on my head and folded it carefully. My mother tapped my shoulder again and smiled. Everyone was still singing. "Who do you know says cleft?" Bootsie whispered. She sure had a way of getting to the meat of something without mincing a lot of words.

After the singing, four men in black suits walked down the center aisle holding gold bowls, and everybody put money in them. My mother put in a dollar and gave Carole, Bootsie, and me each a quarter. Bootsie and I dropped our quarters in at the same time and they made a loud bong against the side of the bowl. My mother gave us a dirty look and we lowered our heads. Bootsie nudged my leg, so I glanced out of the corner of my eye. She was smiling, so I knew she wasn't any more sorry than I was.

When we were leaving, I planned to light a candle for Mama Cope but there wasn't any. I didn't even bother to ask why. I was just happy to get out of there. My father was waiting outside in the car, so we all got in and went home.

After we had changed out of Sunday clothes into regular clothes my mother announced that we were going to visit the Weldins. My father was doing work for people by that name, so I was eager to know more. When Bootsie and I were alone, I said, "Do they have kids?"

Bootsie laughed and told me that George and Charlie,

their first names, are really, really, really old, and that King George of England gave their family land in Delaware, which used to be Pennsylvania, because he needed more money to kill the French. "They're rich but like acting poor," she said. She went on to say they wear dirty clothes and have an outhouse, where pee and poop falls into a hole in the ground, and that Harry, the oldest brother, got himself stuck to the outhouse seat and froze to death, pooping.

"When you get old your skin gets thin and sticks to things," she explained.

"No way!"

"Way!"

When I smiled, she took it as a win, and continued her story. She told me that Harry was frozen solid and Daddy had to hook up a hair dryer and blow hot air to free him from the seat. When the ambulance people came they couldn't get his knees to straighten, so they let him ride up front and Cousin Tommy watched the whole thing.

"Who's he?"

"Our cousin."

I could see that Bootsie wasn't going to make this easy.

"Does he live there, too?" I said, determined.

"In the outhouse?"

"With the Weldins?"

"No, he lives with his parents."

"Where?"

"Behind the Weldins near the trolley barn. His dad is Daddy's brother. His mom is Ukrainian. She doesn't expect much because everyone in the Ukraine is starving – that's what Daddy says. One night I saw her in the trolley barn, hiding, because Uncle Frank was drunk again."

For a long moment, I stood there trying to decide what piece of the family puzzle I should ask about next. Bootsie had a different idea. She leaned towards me and said, "Tell you a secret if you promise not to tell anyone."

"Okay, I promise," and I crossed my heart to seal it.

Bootsie glanced over both shoulders, then she put her mouth close to my ear and whispered. "Down the lane from them is a burned-out mansion. Even the front steps are gone ... but I got in."

She paused, then checked over both shoulders again. "Guess what I found in there?"

"How should I know?"

A guarded look came onto her face and she said, "Nudie magazines."

"Naked?"

"Totally."

"Men too?"

"Yep."

"Ugh! Who do you think they belonged to?"

Bootsie shrugged. "Most were in French. One had a picture of a naked girl sitting on a motorcycle drinking a milkshake. Want to go with me?"

I gave it some thought, "Okay."

A short time later, we heard a car start up. I glanced out the window and saw my mother and Carole with a picnic basket and a large Thermos.

"BOOTSIE ... BETSY." My mother's voice sounded urgent. "Outside."

Bootsie and I did as we were told. The back seat was covered with a canvas drop cloth and smelled of paint thinner. Bootsie and I pushed the cloth to the floor. But we were soon sorry because it let off more dust than a busted vacuum cleaner. Once the car started moving Bootsie took some napkins out of the picnic basket and wiped the seat, but it didn't do any good because there was too much dust.

"They're wasting napkins," Carole hollered from the front seat.

My mother sneaked a quick glance over Carole's shoulder at us. "Don't start," she warned. "Or we'll just turn the car around and go home."

Bootsie waited until the coast was clear, then she said, "Tattletale," under her breath.

Carole rolled her eyes and said something, but I couldn't catch what she was saying. But Bootsie must have because she gave Carole the most disgusting look imaginable.

When we finally reached the Weldins', I wondered if all the sweating I was doing was somehow playing tricks on my eyes. The house was made of stone and had deep-set windows with long strips of masking tape covering cracks in the glass. The tape went every which way. But from a distance it resembled a bunch of crosses; each with one short arm and one long arm. Sort of the way a cloud can look like a teapot or a French poodle or a face, but it's still a cloud.

On the ground, standing in some low grasses near the front door, was a six-foot statue of the Blessed Mother. "Beautiful," I said, remembering the sweet-looking statue of Mary in St. Peter and Paul Church.

I watched as everyone's eyes narrowed on Mary's face, but none of them replied.

My father parked and we followed him to the front door. He turned the knob and we all stepped inside. "I'm family."

"Except where money's involved," my mother said, almost to herself.

"These things take time." As my father spoke, in the

back of my head I saw Harry sitting in the outhouse and my father aiming a hairdryer at him. I started to laugh, but Bootsie nudged me and my laugh came out as a cough.

"Ssshhh." I wanted to ask why, but Bootsie's eyes warned against it. Not now, they said.

In a small room with a potbelly stove and a low ceiling, George and Charlie were sitting on straight wood chairs. Both men had long legs and long arms and looked poor.

"How's this hot weather treating you?" My father sounded so cheerful you'd have thought it was Christmas, all of a sudden.

I could tell by their expressions George and Charlie had heard what my father said. But instead of answering, George came up with a question of his own.

"What'd you bring to eat?" As he was talking, he stretched one leg straight out and pushed the picnic basket under his chair. Then he pointed his eyes at Charlie and added, "Go out and pump us some water."

Charlie opened his mouth to speak but my mother saved him the trouble. "I brought you some fresh iced-tea."

Nobody said anything further. But you could tell that everybody was trying to come up with something worth saying, especially my father. His eyes moved side to side in his head as if he was writing all sorts of things in there.

I used the silence as a go-ahead to look the place over. The inside was even older and more run-down than I had imagined. In some loose way it reminded me of Lafayette's headquarters at Brandywine Battlefield. I went there on a school bus trip once. Both places were a couple of hundred years old and had wood plank floors and walls as thick as watermelon. But from my observation, Lafayette sure kept a better house. The Weldins owned lots of junk and what wasn't junk looked like junk because it was either rusted or had dust as dense as mold sticking to it. The sofa was the color of a worn-out dollar bill. It wouldn't have surprised me one bit if Old King George himself had popped out of all that mess just to round things out, so to speak.

The windows in the room, there were two of them, were propped open with paint stirrers. It didn't help, though. The air that came in was as hot as what we already had. The only ones who didn't seem to mind were Charlie and George. They crossed their ninety-year-old legs and talked about how they got the Blessed Mother free when a tombstone maker knocked her over by accident, leaving her with only one good arm.

Halfway through the story, Bootsie whispered. "Here we go again."

I covered my smile with my hand.

Minutes later after both brothers had had their say, George stood up. I could tell by the way he held his hands on his hips he was a born know-it-all. And in no time flat he proved me right.

"Mary was my idea." George locked his eyes on his brother as he spoke. "Charlie said it wasn't fit for Methodists to have idols . . . people might mistake us for Catholic. But I told him Mary didn't cost us a blessed penny and it was high time we had a pretty woman around."

I sat with my lips sealed, but inside I was wondering why Protestants hated Catholics so much.

"Pay attention," Bootsie whispered, as Charlie hobbled to the window and stuck his head out. "He's about to talk to Mary."

I could feel my father watching me, but I was afraid to look. Afraid I might set him off again. I stared at the floor, instead.

"Help your mother with lunch and try not to hurt yourself again." As he spoke, my father stepped behind me and ground his knuckles in my back. My body lurched forward, instinctively.

"What's to eat?" George yelled over my head to my father.

"Tuna fish sandwiches," my father yelled back. Bootsie used the distraction to pull me towards the kitchen, where we put sandwiches and napkins on a tray.

"Two each," Bootsie said. "Make sure they don't sneak any extra."

Even though I was embarrassed and my back hurt, I guess the remaining parts of me were okay because I let out a tiny laugh. I had never met rich people who were living like poor people and too greedy to recognize it.

Bootsie hid one sandwich under the napkins and laughed. Out of the corner of my eye I saw my mother looking at us, frowning.

"Do unto others as you would have them do unto you," she said, and Bootsie put the sandwich back with the others.

George met us halfway through the dining room and put one sandwich in his pocket and held another to his mouth and took a bite.

My mother handed Charlie his two sandwiches as George watched. "You girls go eat outside if you want," she said. "In the basket there's a paper bag with your sandwiches and some crackers for the ducks."

"It's too hot out," Carole whined.

"Stop the whining . . ." That's all my mother got out before my father finished her thought. "Or go sit in the car." He kept smiling at Charlie and George; they kept eating.

"I didn't do nothing," Carole said.

"Anything," my mother corrected.

"Listen up I'm putting you in charge." My father's eyes were on my eyes but his words were directed at Bootsie. "Don't wander off, understand?" he said, and Bootsie stood at attention. "Aye, Aye," she saluted.

My father returned her salute with one of his own. "Carry on," he said, and a wide grin came onto his face.

Outside, Bootsie fisted the paper bag and yelled. "Race you."

Her feet didn't wait for an answer; they took off running and kept going. My feet followed and when they got to the pond Bootsie and I were toe to toe, so to speak.

"Tie," I said, panting.

"Tie," she said, and I noticed she wasn't even breathing hard. We threw crackers on the ground and watched two ducks eat. Then a pair of geese pushed the ducks out of the way, honking. "Geese marry for life." She had a smirk on her face, so I said I already knew that and she said I didn't and I told her to shut up and she said, "The truth hurts," and she was right, so I nodded my head and we kept walking.

On both sides of the dirt lane tall sycamores shaded us from the sun. We stopped to pick pebbles out of our shoes, and then walked some more. We took our time so we would see everything and not scare the rabbits and frogs that crossed the lane every so often.

A short distance later I saw a house the size of a garage and in the front yard there was a garden as big as the house and it had rows of geraniums, zinnias, marigolds, pansies, daylilies, and behind them stood rows of sunflowers almost as tall as I was. And, at the end of one row was a doghouse with a black and white dog sticking his head out, asleep.

"That's Spot," Bootsie said, and pointed across the lane

to a long building with part of its roof missing. "And that's the trolley barn I told you about."

Just then I happened to glance up. Sitting in the thickest branches of the tallest tree was a giant slab of marble as if it had been born there.

"I'm climbing up."

"Don't fall."

That was all I had to hear to get me climbing up that tree as if my life depended on it.

"Hey, there's Aunt Mary," Bootsie said, pointing my head in the right direction.

A doll-sized woman was standing near the doghouse. Her hand was raised and waved back and forth above her head.

We waved back, and she turned and went inside.

I blinked my eyes and suddenly I was on stage in a fancy theater and the trees were people clapping and the sun was a spotlight shining on my brand-new tap-shoes and my brand-new dress with pink sequins.

"Whoops." I dropped my sandwich into the tall grasses and kept dancing.

Bootsie pushed a big piece of sandwich into her mouth.

"Time to go," she said between chews.

I was in good spirits, so I did three curtsies for my audience and climbed down. From the house across the lane I heard a door open and then Aunt Mary appeared with a giant brownie for each of us.

"You must be Betsy," she smiled, and looked into my eyes as if she wanted to say a whole lot more, but wasn't quite sure how to say it.

"Nice to meet you," I smiled back.

"I'll get some fresh lemonade." And with that she walked into the house and came out moments later with two glasses of lemonade, with a slice of lemon straddling the rim of each glass. It was almost too pretty to drink. But we were thirsty, so we drank the lemonade straight down and said our good-byes.

Neither of us spoke until we got to the mansion. It was just as good because Aunt Mary was laying heavy on my mind. She reminded me of a fairy, who grows flowers and bakes sweets because it's all she knows.

The mansion wasn't really a mansion. It was just a big, burned-out house with tons of ivy on it and black wood where the windows and doors used to be. Outside was a *No Trespassing* sign written with black paint.

"Was anybody home when it caught fire?"

"Why, are you scared?"

I responded by pulling my legs into what used to be the living room. The room had a brick fireplace and mustard-colored wallpaper stained black from the fire.

I tapped Bootsie on the back. "Where?"

She pushed my hand away. "Follow me."

We went down a long hallway and up a staircase with a wide marble banister that looked as if it might have been really beautiful at one time.

I was thinking about that when I heard Bootsie yell, "Careful of the hole in the last step."

I saw the hole just in time.

Upstairs we went into a small room, and there in the middle of the floor was a pile of magazines a foot high. The magazine on top had a picture of a girl with blond hair and bare breasts, smoking a cigar.

"Look at her tits," Bootsie said. "They're gargantuan."

Mama Cope told me it's a sin to use dirty words. I didn't know if tits was a dirty word, but it sounded like one. I looked up and Bootsie's eyes and mine met.

"What's wrong?"

"Nothing." I reasoned this was no time to start explaining my likes and dislikes, so I brought the conversation to a close.

After looking around, Bootsie pointed to a can of Prince Albert tobacco with a pack of matches inside. On the cover was written, "Roadside Diner."

"Who do you think this stuff belongs to?"

Bootsie picked up the can. "You know as much as I do."

"UGh!" she said, leafing through a magazine. When she got to a picture of a naked man and woman, she held it up. "Men look like they got turkey gobblers." She started laughing and I started laughing, too. I'd never seen a man naked before, but I had to admit she was right about them resembling gobblers.

We looked at a lot more pictures, but they all looked about the same as the first one. By then I had decided that men look a whole lot better in clothes than they do without them.

"We better . . ."

"Ssssshhhh." I stopped Bootsie short because I thought I heard footsteps.

Bootsie's eyes got as big as saucers. Neither of us moved. Then I heard footsteps climbing up the stairs and I thought my heart was going to crash through my chest. Bootsie was trying to look calm, but I knew she was as scared as I was.

"Dog?" she whispered.

It was my father. He walked into the room with his chest moving up and down like a runner looking for air. His eyes were on Bootsie.

"I thought I put you in charge." He held his chest and took a deep breath, then continued. "Both of you out. This place could collapse any second."

Bootsie hung her head, ashamed. "C'mon," she whispered, and we made our way outside and back to the dirt lane. A few minutes later my father joined us. He told Bootsie to run ahead and tell Mommy we lost track of time.

He didn't say a word about the girlie magazines. Not right then, anyway. He waited until Bootsie was out of sight, then he ran the tips of his fingers up my arm and whispered, "You're prettier than any of them."

I sensed something awful was brewing inside of his head, so I started walking faster. He stepped in front of me and cut me off.

"Hey, where's the fire? Most women love to be told they're pretty."

"No." The word fell out of my mouth before I could stop it.

"Wrong answer," my father said, digging his fingers into my arm, "after everything you've put us through."

All of a sudden, I realized that my father blamed me for a whole lot of things I knew nothing about. I dropped my head and blinked my eyes a few times to keep from crying. Then my father's hand lifted my chin, slowly, and his knees bent, and his shoulders rolled forward as he pressed his lips against mine. "Kiss me," he said, and I felt his tongue in my mouth.

I kept blinking, but it was too late. Tears streamed down my face. "Don't, please," I begged. "That's the way you kiss your sweetheart."

"You are my sweetheart," he whispered, and took a handkerchief out of his pocket and patted my eyes. "This'll be our little secret."

Farther up the lane Aunt Mary was working in her garden.

"What time'll Frank be home?" As my father spoke, I turned sideways, so he couldn't see my face. "Not sure," Aunt Mary said, but her eyes were on me. "Please stop back." I smiled and she smiled, too.

Just ahead, my mother was walking towards us, singing as if everything was hunky dory. That was the scariest part.

"Things can get better or worse." My father spoke through clenched teeth like ventriloquists do. "It's all up to you."

VII

Daughters of Pocahontas

The last day of June it rained cats and dogs. With the porch roof over our heads like a giant umbrella, Bootsie and I watched sheets of water wash down the street and pour into potholes and pour back out.

"Let's jump puddles."

"No way, our bodies are temples for our souls."

I thought my ears were going bad on me.

"What?" I said, but inside I was thinking that she was a whole lot more Baptist than she had let on that day we went to church.

"Reverend Profitt says . . ." Bootsie stopped short to point out a barrel floating towards the back end of Woody's lot, where the land dropped off and houses made of cinderblock, without basements, lined up on both sides of the street. "If this keeps up we might get another flood."

"Can you swim?" It was the first thing that popped in

my mind so I said it.

"Heck nobody around here knows how to swim except maybe Sarah and Jean Ann." She paused to open the door and let a cool breeze shoot in, and then she continued. "One time Mr. Benson drove us to Canby Pool but Sarah and Jean Ann refused to get in because they said nigger kids pee in it. Mr. Benson said that was just Mrs. Benson talking but it didn't do any good because Sarah and Jean Ann still wouldn't get in. They spread themselves out on towels like two beached whales and burned themselves to a crisp. You should've seen them. They were more purple than red and could hardly move their legs to walk."

Bootsie fanned her face with her hand. "Another thing," she whispered, "if Mommy knew they call colored people that she wouldn't let us play with them."

I liked playing with them because it got me out of the house, but I also agreed with my mother.

"Anyway," Bootsie continued. "Jean Ann must have seen me grinning at the way she was walking because she said, 'At least we didn't swim in pee.' I was about to let her comment pass and I would have, too, but Jean Ann never knows when to quit. She pulled my towel loose from my arm and threw it on the cement. 'Pick it up,' I ordered, and it damn near killed her but she did. 'Could be right,' I allowed. 'But at least I'm not the one limping around like a cooked lobster with two bad legs.'"

I laughed, and Bootsie continued. "Not more than two weeks after that when Sarah and Jean Ann were shedding the last of their burned skin and looking almost human again, Hurricane Hazel arrived and it rained, just like now, only better, and the creek swelled up and water poured every which way."

"Rain, rain go away. Come on back some other day."

"Are you listening?"

I stopped singing.

"For six days it rained." She pointed at the cinderblock houses. "Red Cross people came and were pulling people out windows into boats."

"Holy cow." I was eager for more details.

"Guess what else?" Bootsie was urging me to trudge on so she could watch me go under a few times before she told me whatever it was I was supposed to already know, but didn't, of course.

"Just continue." My voice sounded annoyed because I was. And seeing how she was grinning from ear to ear didn't make things any easier. She was like a man trying to reel in a forty-pound fish with a bad pole. She watched me for a moment to see if I was going to take her bait; and when I didn't, her grin faded some, but she managed to hold on and keep grinning just long enough to say, "Loud Chevy."

Suddenly a light went on in my head and I remembered seeing Boy Boy's car in the back yard, not twenty feet from where Mrs. Samson chained Coco to the magnolia tree, so I held my hand up and said: "Flooded, right?"

Bootsie stared at me for a moment and her grin faded some more until it wasn't hardly a grin at all, more like a frown with some rounded corners to it. I began to feel sort of bad, knowing how much she enjoyed milking a story, and I had robbed her of the best part.

"You really know how to get on my nerves." She took a deep breath and blew the air out slowly, and when she was done, her grin began to brighten up some, but I could see she had to work at it. Her forehead was pulled down over her eyebrows and her lower lip was quivering, not real bad, just enough to tell me that something peculiar was going on inside that head of hers, and she was having considerable trouble with it.

"I get on *your* nerves?" Sarah and Jean Ann showed up before Bootsie could respond. They were standing in the middle of the street, running in circles, like two dogs chasing their own tails. That was to let us get a good look at their bathing suits. They were the new, two-piece kind that everybody was wearing. I hate people like that. Rita Rosini used to do the same thing, act as if she had to show off everything she owned to the entire world.

We stepped onto the porch. The cool air felt good on my hot skin. "I hope their stupid bathing suits fall down," I said.

Bootsie didn't answer but I could tell she was thinking more or less the same thing. I attributed her smug smile to the fact that Jean Ann's stomach rolled over her bathing suit like a lump of warm bread dough. When Jean Ann jumped, her stomach jumped, too, only it landed a little bit later than the rest of her did. It was a beautiful thing to watch because it evened things out, so to speak. I mean we didn't have new suits and Jean Ann looked awful, so all in all we felt pretty good about ourselves.

"C'mon." Bootsie took my hand and we stepped back inside.

That's when it happened. A sudden shift in the wind blew a spray of water right at us. We ducked, but the water came in through the screen and soaked us to the bone.

Bootsie dried her face on my shirt. Her cowlick, which rose like the spout of a teapot over her high forehead, was dripping water, drop by drop, onto my arm. For a brief moment I thought about flattening her hair, but she must have been reading my thoughts because she grabbed my arm in mid-air and yelled, "Don't."

I pulled my arm free, faking anger. "Next time dry your face on your own shirt."

Bootsie stared at her feet as if they knew something she didn't, or shouldn't talk about at least. I said a few words, I don't remember what, as I watched a soda bottle wash into a pothole and spin in slow circles like the hands on a clock.

"Did you hear me?" For a split second I didn't even realize it was my voice, but then Bootsie said, "It's *my shirt*," so I picked up from there. "I'm bored."

I decided to wait her out and while I was waiting, I said a silent prayer that she wasn't going to say anything about that day at the burned-out mansion.

"Ummmm." That's all she said, but after she said it she took a deep breath. Then her mouth closed, opened, and closed again. You would have thought she was about to recite the Ten Commandments with all the hemming and hawing she was doing.

Finally, she cleared her throat about twenty times and got straight to the point.

"Do you like living with Mama Cope or here better?"

I could tell by her tone of voice that she was fishing for a certain answer, so I gave it to her.

"Here."

"Do you mean it?"

"Sure."

"Good." When Bootsie spoke, her eyes lit up like a pinball machine with a new nickel. And when I saw that, I didn't feel one bit guilty about saying 'here' when I should have said 'there.' People say that telling the truth is easy, but it's not so. I have always found you can hurt somebody just as quick with the truth as you can with a lie. Anyway, that's been my experience.

"ONE. TWO. THREE," Sarah and Jean Ann shouted. Then they jumped over a large puddle. At least that's what they were attempting to do, only Jean Ann never got to the other side because her foot slipped from under her and she landed flat on her back. Sarah pulled on Jean Ann's arms and begged her to get up, but Jean Ann screamed and hollered and said she couldn't move because her legs didn't work anymore.

Bootsie ran down the steps, then me. A sheet of rain hit us face-on like a spray of ocean without the salt. Our hair flew every which way and our shoes filled up with water. I glanced over at Bootsie. If she was worried about her soul, she didn't let it slow her feet down any. "Coming," she yelled.

Bootsie and I got behind Jean Ann and we were about to grab her arms, when all of a sudden, a cement truck appeared out of nowhere, and Jean Ann jumped up as if somebody had just given her a brand new pair of legs. Well, Bootsie and I laughed until we almost peed ourselves, then we ran back onto the porch and stepped inside.

In the kitchen we dried our faces on a dishtowel, then hung it on the back of a chair.

"Finish telling me about Boy Boy's car."

Bootsie spread peanut butter on her tongue with a knife and laughed. Again I was reminded of how easily she could get on my nerves.

"Okay, just before the storm hit I heard Woody tell Boy Boy to move his car up the street to higher ground. But he said he wanted it right where it was so he could keep an eye on it. And that's what he did, only I didn't see him doing it because a little later the wind kicked up and Daddy made all of us go in the dining room and lie face down along the wall where the potbelly stove used to be because he said it was the strongest part of the house."

Bootsie knifed more peanut butter and waited for me to say something so she could guage my reaction. I started counting in my head: 10, 9, 8, 7, 6 . . . I was on 5, when she continued talking. "Outside looked like an Alfred Hitchcock movie. Tree branches were flying every which way and the sky was black because the rain was so thick and all."

"What happened to Boy Boy's car?"

"Don't rush me I'm getting there," Bootsie said, smacking her lips. "Anyway, we could hear the wind getting stronger and stronger. When we finally stood up Boy Boy's car was on its side and tree branches were all over it. Two hubcaps were missing, maybe all four, but I couldn't really see because the sky was still black and the water was getting higher."

"Wow!"

"You should have seen when Boy Boy came running out of his house wearing a pair of big fishing boots. He yanked open one of the doors and climbed in like he was getting ready to go for a ride. Only he forgot about the car being on its side and the next thing I knew he was sliding across the seat and sitting behind the steering wheel and honking the horn like crazy. That's when Woody yelled, "Cut the racket," and Boy Boy crawled out a window.

Bootsie poured a glass of Kool-Aid and took a gulp. "Boy Boy tried pushing the car right side up. But the water was clear up to his knees and his feet kept going out from under him. Mommy and Carole didn't watch because they didn't want to. But Daddy nearly laughed himself to death, and it was funny, only I didn't laugh. I was about to, but at that very moment, Boy Boy began crying like a baby and it took all the fun right out of it."

Bootsie searched my face for a long moment. Then in

a small voice, almost too small to make out the words, she whispered, "Do you think I look like a boy?"

The question seemed to appear out of nowhere and I wasn't sure where to go with it.

"Of course not," I heard myself say. "You just need a new hair-do. I cut Rita's."

Bootsie tucked a loose strand of hair behind her ears and a slow smile came onto her face. "I want a page boy."

"Get me a picture," I said, and we shook hands on it.

"Back to Boy Boy," Bootsie said. "The next day his car got towed and when it came back it looked brand new like nothing ever happened."

"Oh." I kept my answer short, not because I didn't like the story; I liked it just fine. Even so, I had to admit it would have been a lot more interesting if the wind had been blowing the right way and Boy Boy's car had gotten a whole tree, instead of two branches.

"Okay," she said. "What's wrong?"

"Nothing."

She took my hand and folded her fingers into mine. "When it stops raining wanna go arrowhead hunting?"

"Is it far?" I made my voice sound flat to offset the smug look she was wearing. I could tell she was about to go into one of her Indian lessons, and she did.

"Running Fawn must learn the lay of the land like the deer and coyote."

I wanted to pick out my own Indian name, but I decided to think things over. And while I was thinking, Bootsie talked about the differences between Indian dirt and other dirt and I got to wondering how many times Chief Joseph was forced to listen to things that didn't make sense. Mama Cope once told me he was a man of patience, which in her estimation was hard to acquire and even harder to hold onto.

By late afternoon Bootsie was done drawing a map that had plenty of arrows for directions, and decided to teach me how to dig without hurting arrowheads and other stuff that might be hidden underneath. She put some hairpins and buttons and a few Frosted Flakes in a bowl of flour and had me search for them with a Popsicle stick. It seemed like a lot of work for nothing being how I was an experienced gardener. But I didn't say anything because I knew she would find some hole in my argument to go on about. So I dug and scraped and I guess I did a good job because when I found the last hairpin, she said I was ready to go arrowhead hunting.

"Not in this rain," my mother called from the dining room. "Play a game. I'm sure Carole would love to play charades."

"Would not." Carole's voice came out of nowhere.

"Teepee," Bootsie said, and we threw a sheet over the dining room table.

And while I set up camp, Bootsie telephoned Sarah and Jean Ann. Minutes later there was a honk outside and Sarah and Jean Ann came running in, umbrellas first.

"Welcome kimosabes," Bootsie said, and we stared in disbelief.

Sarah and Jean Ann were wearing dresses that their mother made for them that looked as near perfect as two dresses can look. Bootsie said the only Indians that ever wore dresses as nice as those dresses fit must have lived on some plantation way down south. Bootsie and I wore trousers made out of potato sacks and they itched like crazy, but they looked like real Indian pants.

"The Great Spirit is with us," Bootsie said. Then she began to teach us a ceremonial rain dance she saw on "The

Lone Ranger." She said if we danced just right we could get as much rain as we wanted. Of course, she wanted a flood. First she did the dance, and then we did it. Then she did it again. But Sarah and Jean Ann couldn't get it right because they kept tripping on their fancy dresses.

Finally, Bootsie signaled us to stop. "I'll start over and go real slow," and she did the dance again, start to finish and we followed.

This time Jean Ann fell. And when she got up Bootsie announced that due to unforeseen technical difficulties, our lesson was postponed.

"What are we gonna do now?" Sarah wanted to know.

Jean Ann tied the sash around her waist in a giant bow. "Our mother didn't drive us over here to sit around and do nothing."

Bootsie chewed on her lip for a minute.

"I got it," she said, and her eyes brightened. "Let's start our very own Indian club." This was the only way, she said, we were ever going to learn to act like real Indians. Everybody thought it was a swell idea.

"The Daughters of Pocahontas." I suggested the name and Sarah seconded it, so I wrote the name down on paper and made it official.

"Anyone joining has to sign up," Bootsie said.

Sarah and Jean Ann signed and Bootsie charged twenty-five cents each for membership dues. She said it was only right we paid up, too, so that night she got fifty cents from my father and put it in the wampum box. We asked Carole to join but she said she wouldn't be caught dead in any club of ours. Then Bootsie and I did the rain dance and climbed into bed happy.

"That's better," Bootsie said, pushing the wampum box under her bed.

I wanted to believe her, so I did.

"Whoops, I forgot something," and with that, I got out of bed because Mama Cope said if you don't brush your teeth, they fall out.

In the bathroom I was squeezing Colgate on my toothbrush when my mother's voice came through the floor register. "The rent is late . . . again."

"Don't nag." My father's voice was loud and angry. "I put up with enough shit at work, I don't need more."

"SSShhhhh, lower your voice," my mother whispered. "Carole's sleeping."

"She belongs upstairs."

"You know there isn't room."

"Not my fault. You changed everything, not me."

"Bill, for God's sake, this isn't about Betsy. For once just tell the truth."

"Careful . . . I warned you . . . leave my mother out of this. Another thing, tell that Reinheart woman to lose our number. She can burn the goddamn clothes for all I care."

Tears rolled down my face and fell through the floor register.

No, I mouthed. They're *mine.*

VIII

Blood Sisters

Bootsie popped the screen out of the kitchen window and stuck her head out.

"Sun's out," she announced.

The sky, which had been the color of eggplant for most of the week, had turned blue somewhere in between the time I won my second game of checkers and was threatening to make it three in a row.

I juggled two of her men I had won only moments before. "You playing or not?"

Bootsie was red. "Fire before ashes," she snapped.

I told her to sit down or the next time we played I would be red.

She fell into her chair with such a thud the table shook. "Roll your eyes all you want," she said, and I did just that. "Red's *my* lucky color."

Then she went on to explain how colors are somehow connected to a person's astrological sign and depending on what moon the person is born in and what star she falls under, certain colors give her special powers. I told her it was hogwash.

As I spoke, my fingers slid in my pocket and through the loops of Rita Rosini's ribbon. "*Mala occhi*," I whispered, just in case any evil spirits were around and I couldn't see them.

"Talk normal," Bootsie ordered and jumped one of my men.

Then she wiped sweat off of her face with a napkin and studied the board. Her men were trapped. "Don't take all day, I got things to do."

"Me, too," I said, and she went on talking. And while she talked, I sent my black men down the board and made kings out of every one of them. And once they were crowned, they gobbled up her red men quicker than King Henry gobbled up wives. Sister Mary Kathryn, my fifth grade teacher, told us all about him. She said King Henry was the meanest man who ever lived. And if we ever heard somebody say different, we would know that that person was Protestant. Mary Eppes said she didn't know what Protestant was so Sister Mary Kathryn explained it. She said Protestant was what King Henry called himself after the pope got mad at him for killing all his wives. Rita Rosini was Protestant but she never killed anybody.

"Got something to tell me?" Bootsie's voice cut through my thoughts like a fast train cutting through fog.

I kept my eyes on the board and my mouth shut. I knew either one might give me away if I wasn't extra careful.

"Earth to Betsy. Come in Betsy."

"I don't know what you're talking about."

"Yes, you do."

"Think whatever you want."

"Don't act like a jerk."

I didn't answer. One of my kings had a clear shot at two of her men and took them, easy as pie, one right after the other.

Bootsie spread her hands over her remaining men to keep my kings from getting to them.

"You're cheating," I said, and moved one of my kings backwards.

Bootsie nodded her head and grinned as if she had something important to say but was holding back, waiting for just the right moment. I could feel sweat inching down my neck onto my back. I looked away. I was afraid if she saw my face she would know I was thinking about that burned-out mansion again.

"Don't lie . . ." she began, and for a brief moment, I felt my heart stop but I was still breathing, so I knew I wasn't dead. Then she said, "Crown me," and I felt my heart start back up.

She grabbed a red checker out of my hand. "Crown me!" she repeated, but her joy didn't last long. "Rats, how did that happen?"

I acknowledged the situation with a nod. Her men couldn't move any which way without one of my black men jumping them. She saw this, too. I could tell by the way she was shifting her feet. That's when I started humming. I hummed while my men jumped. When they were done, I juggled two of her men and hummed some more. I was still humming, when, all of a sudden, I felt my chair give way and she was on top of me pounding me with her fists. I reared up and pushed her off. But before I could get to my feet, she was on top of me again.

"Get off, bozo," I screamed.

"Not until you tell the truth, the whole truth, and nothing but the truth."

And just like that my old life ended and my worse nightmare was staring me in the face in the middle of broad daylight. I didn't want to talk, period. So I said, "I already told you, 'I don't know what you're talking about.'"

"Liar." Bootsie spit the word out like some ballplayers spit out stale chewing tobacco. And this time she forced my arms over my head and pinned them to the floor. I reared up again, but it was useless.

"Leave me ALONE," and I made sure all Delaware heard me.

"You girls stop that fighting," my mother called from the back yard where she was hanging out wash.

A minute or so passed and Bootsie got a troublesome look on her face. I could tell that she had decided I wasn't ever going to give in, no matter what. I fixed my eyes on her eyes and stared like a crazy person, without blinking or anything. Rita Rosini said I had Bette Davis eyes and one day I could play a crazy woman in the movies if I wanted to.

More minutes passed, lots of them. I could feel my strength return. It felt good. Mama Cope was right. About being stubborn, I mean.

"Do you give up?" I had almost forgotten Bootsie was on top of me.

"Never." I said the word real slowly.

"You're hopeless," she groaned, and finally let me up.

I looked at her the same way George Washington must have looked at Benedict Arnold when he discovered that things between them were a lot different than he had imagined.

"I hate you," I said.

Bootsie began to shift her feet, so I knew she heard me, but she didn't say anything. Finally, she moved one of her men back a space. It was a bad move. One of my kings gobbled up both her kings and two other men.

She only had three men left and two of them had my kings breathing down their necks. I knew I had her so I smiled real wide. Of course, it was a fake smile.

She lowered her thumb onto a checker and held it there. A minute passed, then another minute. My jaws were getting stiff from smiling. She lifted her thumb slowly. I could feel my jaws relax and a genuine smile form where the fake smile had been. Her eyes hardened and she pushed the board back and forth with her elbow.

"Stop it." One of my kings slid under the table and disappeared. "I said, 'Stop.'"

She slapped the board onto the floor. "Okay, if that's what you want," she sneered, and walked away.

A whole day passed before we were on regular speaking terms again. Bootsie spoke first. We were watching television at the time.

"Wanna go arrow hunting?" she said as if everything was peachy.

It wasn't. But I pretended it was because she gave in first, and to my way of thinking that was a plus in her column.

"Can Sissy Jupe come?" I said, cushioning my answer with a request.

My father walked in the room and turned off the television.

"It's not safe outside for him," he said, motioning for me to stand up. "Besides, you're coming with me today."

I started for the hall, but my father cut me off and said, "Where do you think you're going?"

"Mommy wants us," Bootsie said, fielding the question before I could get to it.

My father looked puzzled. "For what?"

"Clean our room," she said, calmly as can be.

"Shouldn't take both of you. The room's not that big." My father's knuckles were digging in my back for a response. I bit my lip to keep from crying.

I glanced at Bootsie. I could tell by the look in her eyes that she was ready for him.

"Not fair," she sighed. "I always get stuck with the yucky work."

"Whoa, slow down." My father banged the bowl of his pipe on the windowsill. Clumps of black tobacco fell onto the sill then flew backwards into the room by a light breeze. He blew into the stem of the pipe to clear it. Then he loaded the bowl with fresh tobacco and set it on fire.

"Okay, you can both stay. But the room better be spic-n-span when I get home. You hear me?"

"Yes, sir, Daddy," Bootsie said, and nodded her head triumphantly.

As soon as my father left for work Bootsie announced there were mice in our closet and my mother ordered us to scrub, just like Bootsie predicted she would.

"Rule number one," she said, pouring Pine-Sol into a pail of hot water. "Tell one tell the other."

"Roger dodger." And as I said it, a feeling of sisterhood came over me. I almost said something, but the smell of Pine-Sol rushed up my nostrils and made me sneeze. Bootsie sneezed, too. We laughed and got down on all fours and slapped wet rags on the lineolum like we were chasing mice only there weren't any, of course.

My mother beamed. "Good job."

We wiped sweat off of our faces and moaned like men

in war movies do when the camera is on them. Apparently my father had telescopic eyes and could see us, but we couldn't see him because my mother said, "Your father loves seeing you girls helping out."

Anyway, when the coast was clear we emptied the bucket into the toilet and ran outside. Bootsie carried the map and handed me a walking stick she had whittled into the shape of a golf club, fat end up.

"Howdy ladies." Woody stepped out of his truck, smiling.

"Hi," Bootsie and I said in unison.

Mrs. Hicks opened the screen door. "Around back," she yelled, "and take those dirty shoes off."

Mrs. Hicks seemed to enjoy yelling at Woody. One time I heard her say he was worse than a thousand heathens because he put doing all the Lord's work on her shoulders. She said other stuff, too, about him being a bad role model for Boy Boy and staring at her with his glass eye. Bootsie said it was the Holy Roller in her coming out.

"Yadadada." Bootsie spoke slowly as if she derived some sort of special pleasure from hearing her own voice.

Without bothering to take a breath, she mumbled, "Poor Woody," and proceeded to tell me about the time he offered Boy Boy five dollars to go to a revival meeting that Mrs. Hicks was all excited about. "Well, Boy Boy hemmed and hawed until he got Woody to up the stakes to ten dollars. Then he went. But unbeknownst to Boy Boy Mrs. Hicks had spread the word he had come to be saved. Over and over she raised his name up to God hoping that Boy Boy would hear God's will, for himself, on the way down. Of course, he didn't. Finally, he agreed to be saved but it cost Mrs. Hicks an extra ten whole dollars. She paid it, too. But later I heard Boy Boy tell her he wouldn't go to another revival meeting for a whole wheelbarrow full of money. He never did either."

"His loss," I said, and we both had a good laugh.

When we reached the edge of the woods, she slid the walking stick under my arm and said, "Careful."

In the back of my mind I saw my father pushing me down the porch steps. I raised my arm and the walking stick fell to the ground. As soon as she reached for it I ran behind a big oak tree to prove I could stand on my own two feet just fine, thank you.

"*Bet... sy.*" I watched Bootsie scan the tree line with her eyes. A moment later she showed up and poked the tip of the walking stick into my leg.

"Get that away..." Before I could finish my sentence, Trevor Lester, who lived in an apartment building behind Sarah and Jean's house, and a thin-faced boy with a patch of yellow hair riding low over his eyes, stepped onto the path. I could tell by the look on their faces they were looking for trouble. They rolled their eyes over us and passed a mean grin between them. Then they began to laugh. Bootsie had a serious look on her face. "Let's go," she said.

I didn't move. I followed Trevor's eyes. They were on Bootsie's feet. She had a blue sock on one foot and a green sock on the other and the green sock had a hole in it. I got an awful knot in my belly.

"Looky here, Jimmy." Trevor paused to made sure Jimmy was with him. "She's wearing holy socks."

Jimmy crossed himself in mock prayer.

Trevor laughed and slapped his leg for emphasis. "Must think it's Sunday."

I could feel my blood boiling. I glanced over at Bootsie for instruction but her feet were shifting and her mouth was closed tight. I fixed my eyes on Trevor's eyes and waited for all the laughing to dry up. Then I smiled. The smile came out my eyes, without warning, and was meant more as a threat than a smile.

"Jean Ann told me you're weird," Trevor sneered. "Told me you eat boogers."

Jimmy and Bootsie were staring at the ground, motionless, as if they were in shock. It was just Trevor and me. Whenever my fear started to rise up, I pushed it down with anger and kept smiling.

Another minute or so passed and Trevor got a troubled look on his face. I could tell that he had decided I was crazy so I kept smiling to make sure he didn't change his mind.

Jimmy was the first to speak. "C'mon Trevor, let's go."

"Yeah," Trevor said, walking away. "Weirdoes."

"Booger eaters," I screamed, boring holes through their backs with my eyes.

After they were gone, I took a few quick breaths to calm my nerves and think things over for a moment. I walked towards Bootsie but her feet, dragging in the high grass, moved away. I didn't know what to do when she was like this.

"He's mad he lost yesterday," I said, finally. My father had set up the race, of course. They were running the hundred-yard dash and it looked as if Trevor might win. They were neck to neck the whole way. Then about twenty yards from the finish line, he got a stupid grin on his face and she just happened to glance over and see it. Well, I saw her eyes light up with fire and I knew that was it. She stretched her shoulders forward and ordered the rest of her body to do the same. Then she shifted, like a well-oiled engine, into higher gear. He tried to catch up, but he couldn't. She was standing at the finish line facing him when he came in panting like an old workhorse. The only thing that could have made it better was if Butchie was there, himself. But ever since they got into that fight at Tull's, and the gumball machine broke, Butchie didn't come around much. We still saw him down by the creek fishing. And, once in a while, we saw him riding his bike with friends. At those times he called us queers or maggots. But he never came to Tull's or the Brighton Avenue Track Events again.

"I'm hungry." Bootsie leaned on the walking stick and stepped forward.

I knew she wasn't hungry, but I didn't say anything. I ducked under a low branch, and when we were even, I tapped her arm.

"You okay?" I said, and she nodded.

"Did Jean Ann really say boogers?"

"No, but he didn't deny it. We got them good." I didn't know why she had acted like a baby, but I cut her some slack, and kept walking.

We both laughed, and I saw in her eyes my own eyes. "We got them good," I said and we both fell silent. I didn't know why Bootsie had acted like a sissy, but I cut her some slack and kept walking.

The next day she called an emergency meeting of The Daughters of Pocahontas. "White man has no honor. We Indians must band together."

"Amen," Jean Ann said. "Praise the Lord."

"Phony," I mumbled, just loud enough for her to hear.

"What'd I do?" she growled.

"Ask Trevor."

"Silence," Bootsie ordered. "This is the day of the risen fawns. From this day forward we will band together as sisters and be known among all nations as fawns of the Great Spirit . . . ."

"I want," Sarah began, but Bootsie stopped her.

"First," Bootsie continued, "in order for us to become real Indians we must become blood sisters by cutting our fingers and mixing the blood all together." It was the only way, she said, we would ever be able to think like real Indians.

I brought up the fact we were already sisters but she said I was missing the point. "All that means is we share the same parents. Blood sisters are closer than regular sisters."

"Besides, being blood sisters will give us extra strength to hunt buffalo."

I knew that Bootsie was just saying all this for Sarah and Jean Ann's sake. She was doing her best to make Indians out of those two but I didn't have much faith in them changing.

I was right. The day after we became blood sisters they quit. They said their mother didn't want them joining any club that required cutting their fingers or any other part of them.

"Girls should look pretty," Mrs. Benson told Bootsie and me. Sarah and Jean Ann were standing next to their mother and I noticed they had a big hunk of gauze wrapped around their index fingers. "Just look at their poor hands. I had to bandage them to keep infection from setting in."

Bootsie and I didn't answer. We looked down at our own fingers and besides a tiny little mark where the pin went in, we couldn't find any reason for her concern.

"Wasn't our idea to quit," Jean Ann said the next day. "Mommy noticed blood on Sarah's finger and she made us tell."

I could see in Bootsie's eyes that she didn't believe Jean Ann but she didn't waste any time arguing about it. She was real gracious. "Don't worry about it," she told Jean Ann. "We can play Indians the old way."

But we never did. Bootsie said that once you're blood sisters, you can't go back to being your old self.

"Who needs them? You and I are blood sisters, that's all that counts."

I nodded.

"RUNNING FAWN AND RED FAWN DAUGHTERS OF THE GREAT SPIRIT." As she spoke she took a safety pin out of her pocket, stuck our fingers, and pressed her finger to mine. I watched her blood and my blood run down our skin and collect in our nails.

"Just in case them quitting put a hex on us," she said. "This makes it forever."

IX

Roadside Diner

"Get up." My father's voice caught me off guard. It came with a puff of stale smelling tobacco that fell across my closed eyes. I know my nose moved because I could feel it moving. Leave, I prayed.

"I said, 'Get up.'" My father was leaning over my bed as if he was looking for something and he needed to be extra close to find it. Then I heard feet move, and I imagined the Lord pushing him towards the door.

"You're coming with me." And just like that I knew my prayer had failed. My father squeezed my foot and I swallowed my scream and I was as still as a dead person. But faking sleep was useless because my foot hurt like the dickens. I cracked one eye to check if it still resembled a foot. My father tightened his grip, and I sucked in another scream.

"I know you can hear me," he said, blowing another

puff of tobacco in my face.

I opened my eyes. And when I did, my mouth opened, and a soft moan fell out. My father smiled. It was a mean smile that moved across his face slowly. Suddenly, it occurred to me that I could fake sleep until my foot fell off and my father would be standing there, no matter what. I glanced at Bootsie. Her face was under her arm, which she lifted every so often to sneak a peek.

"She can't save you this time," my father said, and her face disappeared back under her arm.

My nose and throat were full of tobacco smoke. I turned my head and felt something burning my chin. It was his pipe. I pulled my head back and coughed.

My father laughed between puffs. "You said you liked the smell of pipe tobacco."

The words blew out of his mouth real casual-like as if he were saying the honest-to-goodness truth. You would've had to be there to understand how convincing he could be. He was a born storyteller. And somewhere along the line he learned that mixing a little truth in with a handful of lies is the best way to get something over on someone. One time I almost believed one of his lies myself. Not because there was necessarily any truth in it, but because I liked the way it sounded. A lie can do that: make you believe something you want to believe because it's softer to take than the truth. For example, my bat with Mickey Mantle's signature on it. Mickey Mantle didn't really sign it, some machine at a factory did, but it looked like a real signature just the same. My father said he bought the bat because we got off on the wrong foot and he wanted to set things right. It was a lie, of course. What he really wanted was to keep the burned-out mansion a secret. If he had looked at my face he would have known that what happened was too ugly to talk about. But I did keep the bat. It was pretty.

I wrapped my sheet around me and got out of bed. My father's eyes didn't move. They looked like two tiny glazed apples with the cores chewed out of them.

"Excuse me." I waited a moment, then I repeated my request. "Excuse me."

This time he let me pass. That's when it happened. I was halfway out of my blouse when one of my arms got tangled in the sheet and the more I tried to free it, the harder it was to move. I gave the sheet a good tug. For a second or two, I thought I had won. Then I felt warm air from the window on my breasts. I draped my blouse down the front of me and tugged. Finally, the sheet untangled and I covered myself up.

I glanced at Bootsie and her eyes closed. Traitor, I mouthed.

For one brief moment, my anger renewed me. I slid my panties on and yanked my shorts to my waist. Then I dropped the sheet, wiggled my feet into flip-flops, and glanced at Bootsie again. Her eyes were still closed.

"Ready." I used the same sort of voice I imagined a man on death-row uses when he's being strapped into the electric chair and asked to say a few words. I reasoned that most men, given the situation, couldn't get out more than a word or two anyway. But one time Mama Cope told me that she read about some fellow in Georgia or someplace that blabbed up a storm. I never forgot it.

"Outside in two minutes," my father called from the hall. "And don't wake your mother. She needs her sleep."

Drop dead, I mouthed, and brushed my hair up into a ponytail.

"Want me to come?" I could tell by Bootsie's tone that

she wanted me to say, 'no,' so I threw my hairbrush at her, and ran down the stairs without answering. When I got to the dining room, I could hear my father's Ford making a loud choking noise and I kept walking.

"Hurry before he wakes up the entire neighborhood." My mother's voice rose behind me like steam rising from a boiling teakettle. She was on the sofa, where she had slept through the night. It was her way of telling my father he couldn't throw her mother's soup tureen, the one with gold angels on it, across the dinner table and expect her not to retaliate. On her lap was a towel and on the towel was her tureen with glue oozing out of numerous cracks.

My father was on his horn.

"No gerrymandering." Another Scrabble word I didn't know, reminding me that my mother approached life indirectly, never head on. "Today is your turn to clean the bathroom."

"Can I stay?"

"Now now, your father's waiting on you."

I walked to the car and settled myself into the front passenger seat.

"What the hell took you so long?" My father gave the gas pedal a quick push to steady the engine. "C'mon Lulu," he said, and the car jerked, then leaped forward and kept going. "It's almost eight-thirty. We'll be lucky to get a goddamn seat."

When he got to eighty, my father patted the dashboard. "Thata girl," he said, and the needle hit eighty-five.

I dug my fingers into the seat. I thought about jumping out, but cars and trucks were whizzing by and I was afraid I would get run over.

"Hungry?"

I nodded, and my father grinned his stupid Father-

Knows-Best grin.

I closed my eyes and played make-believe. Suddenly, I was with Mama Cope and she was reading the scene where Huck Finn goes to church with Buck and his family and a mess of guns to help everyone listen better. I was laughing. But Mama Cope was frowning. "When people are one way outside and another inside," she was saying, "it's no laughing matter." When I opened my eyes my father was pulling into a parking lot. At one end was a diner that looked like an old railroad car someone had put on a slab of concrete and planted in the middle of nowhere. It was aluminum and had a flat roof. To the side of the door, above a faded Coca-Cola sign, were the words "Roadside Diner."

I don't know why but I kept eyeing that sign as if I'd seen it before or thought I'd seen it before, but I couldn't for the life of me figure out where.

My father parked in the last row under an elm tree with branches that spread over our car like a huge fan. There were a dozen or so other cars and one pick-up in the lot. The closest was a white Dodge. But it was a good ways back and faced the diner. Our car was the only one facing the tree.

"Get out."

The sun was low in the sky and it was hot and getting hotter. Even my feet were sweating. I had to walk extra slow to keep my sandals from sliding off.

When I got inside, my father was already seated at the counter. The diner wasn't fancy but it looked clean enough. The counter was made of white Formica and a green strip of rubber was nailed along the front edge. Halfway down was the biggest cash register I'd ever seen. It was made of iron and weighed about a thousand pounds. It was also covered with a lot of nice, pretty carvings of trees and flowers and birds that almost looked alive except they were made out of metal. I would've stared longer if my father hadn't poked me in the arm and read: "National Cash Register Co. 1889."

I didn't say anything, but I appreciated him pointing the words out. At that moment, I would've done almost anything to be behind that cash register, pushing buttons and watching the drawer open and close.

Anyway, while I was thinking about all this, a man with a receding hairline and a dirty apron dangling from his neck walked over and stood in front of my father.

"If it isn't Bill Toppin," the man said, waving a spatula with one hand and shaking my father's hand with the other. "We all thought you finally won the Irish Sweepstakes and moved on."

My father grinned and the man added: "Who's this pretty little thing you been hiding?"

"This here's Betsy, my youngest."

"Pleased to meet you," the man said, and took my hand in his and squeezed until I couldn't feel my own fingers. I tried to rub some life into them with my good hand, but my father cuffed my wrist and said: "Harry was just being friendly, say, 'Hello.'"

"Hello," I whispered, and my father let go.

Harry turned sideways and that's when I noticed the tattoo of a red and blue snake that seemed to crawl up and down his hairy arm when he talked. The word "Lover" was written in green near the snake's tongue. The tongue was forked and long. It looked as if it wanted to eat "Lover" from the 'L' over to the 'r.'

"Go ahead, touch it." Harry put my hand on the snake's belly and moved it back and forth as if my hand was giving the snake a massage. I tried to pull away, but Harry wouldn't let go of my hand.

"Watch this," he laughed, and made a muscle and a large lump showed up in the snake's belly. He kept flexing and the lump moved up and down as if the snake were alive. I tried to pull back, but Harry resisted.

"It's just a tattoo," my father laughed. "What would you do if you ever saw a real snake?" My father grinned and Harry let go of my hand.

"So Bill, I guess you've been keeping busy."

"Somebody has to bring home the bacon."

Harry winked at me and put two menus on the counter. "The breakfast special is on the cover."

I glanced over the menu and ordered scrambled eggs and scrapple. My father ordered the special: eggs over light, bacon, sausage, home-fried potatoes, toast, and coffee.

"Wish we were busier." Harry speared our order onto a sharp, skinny nail in the wall. "You want them potatoes fried with catsup?"

"Sure, and add some chopped onion," my father said.

"You're the boss." Harry fixed his eyes on my face as he spoke. "This one looks like the wife."

"Stubborn," my father mumbled, more to himself than anyone else.

A tiny woman, with gray hair and a cane, cleared her throat. Then she took her last sip of tea and handed the cup to a young, dark-haired waitress wearing red lipstick and false eyelashes. The eyelashes were so long you couldn't tell if she had real eyebrows or the penciled-on kind.

"My check please, Betty," the woman said, and patted my arm. "You take care," she said.

For a moment it looked as if my father might have

more to say, but if he did he kept his thoughts to himself. When the woman saw that he was done talking, she paid her check and left.

Harry glanced over at Betty who was flipping pancakes on the grill. "Another one," he smirked. "Old and alone."

Betty flipped a pancake onto a plate without answering.

"Don't go getting your tail feathers all ruffled." Harry swatted at a fly on his arm as he talked. It fell to the floor dead.

Betty stared at him, her face a red melon and said, "I'm not in the mood to hear any of your bull-shit."

I was surprised to hear Betty curse in the wide open. But I reasoned that he had asked for it. I wasn't alone because I heard a girl's voice say, "Good for you, Betty."

Harry poked Betty's arm with the spatula. "Move," he said, and slapped an egg and two strips of bacon on a plate and slid the plate down the counter. A short, round-faced man sitting on the stool next to my father stuck his hand out and stopped the plate just short of my father's coffee cup.

"Jesus Christ, Harry," my father said. "Slow down a little."

Betty put my breakfast in front of me.

"Thank you," I said, and cut my scrapple up and ate it.

I was into my eggs when Betty brought my father his breakfast. He poured syrup on his sausage and salted everything real good, but he didn't eat right away. Instead, he talked about how Roosevelt ruined women by giving them jobs. Every so often, he would sweep the counter with his eyes to make sure he hadn't lost anyone. Finally, before anyone had a chance to speak, he finished up with a long-winded commentary.

"Yesterday I heard a woman on the radio say that

buying a pair of nylon stockings with her own paycheck gives her more pleasure than her husband ever did. You should've heard the hoop-la she was making over stockings. You would've thought they were made out of pure gold."

My father cleared his throat as if he were on television and about to say something important. Harry came closer and he cleared his throat again.

"An apple's an apple and an orange an orange." As he spoke my father's face seemed to pull one way and then the other until the fire in his eyes was gone and a soft smile had taken its place. "But, it ain't fair to judge a whole crop by a few rotten ones." He stuffed a forkful of egg and bacon into his mouth. "There are still some decent women out there, just takes more time finding 'em. Like car shopping, same thing. You just need know what you want, check the sticker price, and go from there."

I could tell by the look on Harry's face that all the talk about apples and car shopping had him totally confused. My father saw this as a sign of his superior intelligence and added, "You just worry about cooking." Harry turned and flipped two eggs over lightly and slid them onto a plate and added some homefries and buttered toast. Then he put the plate in front of a man at the other end of the counter. As he walked back our way, he rubbed his forehead like he was thinking things over and reached for my hand. This time I was too quick for him.

"I'm harmless," he laughed.

My father sipped his coffee and shoveled forkloads of food into his mouth without comment. His mouth was so tense I couldn't see his lips, just a straight, hard line marking where his lips used to be. At that very moment, I knew what word was rolling around in my father's head: *moron.*

He used it to describe people who, as he put it, don't have the brain of a jackass.

"Been awhile." The short, round-faced man seated next to my father was talking. "Everything okay?"

"Could be ... should be better," my father said, between chews.

The man tapped his head. "Knock on wood DuPont's been good to me so far."

My father rolled his eyes. He labeled anyone who worked for *The Company* a "sell-out" and claimed that Delaware's chemical giant was loaded with CIA spies. "Careful, Ernie. Every minute you're there, you're being watched."

Ernie kept eating, as if my father had said, "Good eggs."

"That's why I had to get the hell out of there. I knew too much." My father was too busy enjoying himself to notice the shocked looks on faces up and down the counter.

"Nice seeing you," Ernie said, and slid four ones under his saucer. Behind him Betty was ringing up a bill on the cash register. I watched numbers pop up and the drawer open and Betty take some money out and put some money in and close the drawer by pressing her palm against it. If it were mine, I wouldn't put up with all that, especially if people pressed hard and weren't careful.

Betty must have noticed me staring because she said: "Sometime when we aren't busy how'd you like to ring somebody up?"

"Really?" I told myself I'd be careful.

"Sure thing." Betty got a pitcher of cold milk from under the counter and poured me a glass. "On me," she said.

Thank you, I mouthed, as if we were sharing a secret.

As soon as Betty stepped away, my father whispered. "Sit up straight, Bugs."

When I didn't say anything, he glared at me and I

glared back.

"What do you think about that Kennedy fellow?" Harry threw out the question and my father caught it. "Being Catholic, he got a lot of voters worried."

"That so?" A well-dressed man put a dollar on the counter and left.

"Papist," my father said, as Harry walked towards us holding a coffeepot.

"I'll have another cup." When Harry was done pouring, he made a muscle in his arm and the snake started moving again. "Ever see a snake dance?" I shook my head no, and dropped my arms to my sides.

My father put three dollars on the counter and signaled me to stand up. I didn't even get to see Betty ring up our bill and the numbers pop up. On the way out my father reached in a straw basket and took a book of matches. On the front, in black lettering, was written, Roadside Diner. That's when it all came back to me. It was the same name that Bootsie and I found on matches in the burned-out mansion. To me, it could only mean one thing. The matches in the mansion belonged to my father and if they belonged to him the girlie magazines belonged to him, too.

"Get in the goddamn car," my father ordered.

Our car was all alone. Even the white Dodge was gone. I took a deep breath to calm myself, then I climbed into the front seat. I didn't see my father open the driver's door, but I felt his body settle itself behind the steering wheel.

"What the hell?" His voice was low and threatening. "You think I'm blind? I saw the way Harry was looking at you."

I didn't say anything. My eyes were on the windshield. In the back of my head I could hear my father talking, but I can't remember what he said because I was praying that somebody would hear my prayer and save me.

"Come here." My father cupped my breasts in his hands.

"No plea . . ." I began, but he pressed his lips against mine and I couldn't talk. When I tried to pull away, he slid his tongue across my cheek. "No, what?" he laughed.

"No, Daddy," I said, wiping my lips with the back of my hand.

He pinned my arms to the seat. "Don't do that . . . nothing wrong with a little kiss is there?"

"You won't go to Heaven." I don't know where the words came from but that's what I said.

"You sound like I'm a goddamn stranger," he said as if I was doing something wrong and not the other way around. "I'm your father."

Suddenly, a pick-up truck parked alongside us and my father moved back behind the steering wheel.

"Mommy said not to gerrymander because I have to clean the bathroom." As I spoke, two blue jays flew out of the elm tree.

"You better be telling me the truth."

I nodded my head, yes, as we pulled out of the parking lot onto the main road. Then I leaned my head out the window and let the hot summer air blow my hair backwards. It felt good.

X

Charades

When I got home Bootsie was stretched out on the floor in front of the television, steering a cookie shaped like a space ship towards her mouth.

"Stop!" I dove like a blue jay I once saw diving for a cat that had wronged him, headfirst and focused. "It's mine."

Bootsie held on as best as she could but she was no match for my rage. "Give it to me or else."

On the television Rin-Tin-Tin was barking.

"Or else what?" Bootsie laid on each word.

"You'll see." I pounded Bootsie's arm on the floor and the cookie shot straight up and my arm shot up and swatted the cookie towards the sofa.

"There," I snapped.

Bootsie used the distraction to push herself to her feet. "Jerk," she sneered, and squeezed her hand in between the cushions.

"Got it!" The cookie was missing its wings and its nose

was pushed forward making it look more like a kite than a spaceship.

I glared at the cookie, then I glared at her. "I hate … you." The pause did the trick.

For a long moment she just stood there and her mouth fell open and stayed open and her eyes went blank the way fish eyes do when they're out of water. Then her feet started shifting only they were moving and the rest of her wasn't. As usual, I decided to wait her out. I didn't have to wait long.

Her feet anchored themselves and she mumbled, "It was *your* choice. I offered to go with you."

I grabbed the cookie within an inch of her mouth.

"What's wrong with you?" she shouted, as I slid the cookie (now missing its wings, nose and tail) in my pocket.

"YOU … that's what's wrong! I needed you and what did you do … you tell me."

She hung her head and sighed.

"NOTHING!" And with that I threw the broken cookie at her.

She didn't budge. The cookie hit her shoulder and fell to the floor. "I'm sorry," she said.

"I bet you are."

"Wanna do something?"

"Stop changing the subject."

"I'm not."

"Are too."

"I said, 'I'm sorry.'" Being she was the only one in the family I could talk to, it didn't make any sense for me to stay mad, so when she said, "Upstairs," I swallowed my pride and followed after her.

We glanced around for Carole, then I pushed the bedroom knob until I heard the door lock.

"We're alone," Bootsie said, and I breathed a sigh of relief.

A moment later we heard loud music. Boy Boy was coming down the street in his Chevy, with his radio blaring a Little Richard song that had lots of fast-talking piano. I pulled the sheet off of my bed and threw it in big bunches until it covered the window.

"Good idea," she said, and the room went dark. I could feel my heart racing and my chest puff up and down like an inner tube that's letting air in one moment and letting it out the next.

"Good golly Miss Molly, sure like to ball ..." And just like that, she broke into song.

"Traitor," I squeezed in when she finally let up for a breath of air. She plugged her ears with her fingers. "When you're rockin' 'n a' rollin', can't you hear your mama call. From the early, early mornin' til the early, early night ..."

I checked the doorknob.

"It's locked," she said, and unplugged her ears. "Do you think Little Richard is queer?" she added, as if changing the subject mid-stream is perfectly acceptable.

This time I rolled my eyes.

"Sssshhh," Bootsie pushed the sheet to one side to look out the window, "somebody's on the porch."

I could hear voices but I couldn't make out any words. I picked up Sissy Jupe and kissed his head. "You won't ever desert me, huh?"

Bootsie scrunched her face up until her eyebrows climbed up under her cowlick and disappeared. "He's a cat," she snapped.

"No kidding, dodo." I didn't bother to check her reaction because it didn't make a shred of difference to me (at least I told myself that).

We could still hear voices on the porch, so we knew it wasn't safe to talk. Bootsie took a black and white marble notebook out of her underwear drawer and ripped out the first few pages. They had lots of arithmetic problems on them. Then she sat down on the bed and wrote on the cover in red ink, "INDIAN SIGN LANGUAGE" and "SECRET."

"There," she said. I stared at it for a few moments, then I looked her in the eyes and said, "What's that for?"

"Us."

I didn't say anything.

"Indians need to learn how to talk with their hands."

"What if Daddy catches us?"

"Don't worry. We'll pretend we're playing charades. We'll even ask Carole. Then, eventually when it's safe we'll mix in our sign language."

"Carole won't do it."

"Yes, she will. She loves charades. We just won't tell her the sign language part."

I was still leery, but I couldn't help but admire her reasoning. I was tempted to say more but her eyes stopped me.

Trust me, they said.

She began to write. The first page looked like this:

SISTERS	hands together
LOVE	thumb up
GOOD	circle with index finger and thumb
HELP	index finger on cheek
HAPPY	run index finger across mouth
SAD	close eyes touch eyelid with thumb
BAD	shake hand side ways
HUNGRY	point index finger to open mouth
GOD	point straight up
CRAZY	shake head
AFRAID	run finger across neck
DEVIL	point down

"Done," she said, and signaled thumbs up. Then we practiced until we had 'FATHER,' MOTHER,' and 'CAROLE' down and we were on 'SISTERS.' Signing was hard work, but we took our time to make sure we got each word just right.

"As Daughters of Pocahontas we must tell no one."

I gave my word.

"Dinner is ready," my mother called up the stairway.

At the table I kept my hands in my lap and practiced signing. Bootsie nodded, and I nodded back. Then my father arrived wearing new overalls and enough Old Spice to sink the Queen Mary.

Carole sniffed the air like a trained bloodhound.

"You look nice." My mother smiled approvingly.

My father responded by putting ten pounds of dried beef and gravy on my plate. "Eat, it'll put hair on your chest."

My mother shook her head and sighed. "Bill is that kind of talk really necessary?"

My father gripped my wrist and rammed his fork up and down my plate. "Did you hear me, I said, 'Eat.'"

My mother sighed, this time louder. "Not again. We just sat down."

My father let go of my wrist. "You might fool your mother, but you don't fool me ... not by a long-shot."

"Every single meal." My mother dried her eyes with her napkin, and then took a deep breath. "When is this bickering going to end, so we can act like a normal family?"

I stared at my plate, dumbfounded. I hated these talks because they made me feel guilty for being born. I wanted to crawl under the table and disappear. I kept my mouth closed because I knew that if I opened it the truth would come out and I wouldn't be able to stop it. He will never change: NEVER!

"Everything takes time." My mother looked into my eyes as if she could somehow read my thoughts.

My father glanced around the table for support. "What about me? Doesn't anyone care how I feel?"

My mother shoveled dried beef off of my plate back onto the serving platter.

"I know you're trying," she said, and patted my father's hand until he said, "Takes two."

My mother nodded. "Yes, but remember Rome wasn't built in a day."

For the next week I avoided my father and he avoided me. The house was peaceful for a change. My mother sang to the dinner dishes and took to wearing Evening in Paris cologne from morning to night. My father bought it at Tull's when he was buying himself a new corncob pipe.

"Somebody must love you," he crooned when he handed her the cologne. For a brief moment, her eyes brightened and she looked happy. But, as usual, her happiness didn't last. This time my father waited a week before he made his move. Dinner was over and we were about to play Scrabble. To my mother Scrabble was more than a game; it was a way to improve vocabulary, so we would sound erudite, which she explained was another word for educated.

"People notice," she said, turning the wood squares blank-side up. "Don't think they don't."

"I'm intelligence," Carole said, defensively.

"Intelligent," my mother corrected. "It's a noun."

A big grin came onto my father's face. "I tested at 180 . . ."

I was shocked to learn that my father was one of the smartest people in the whole world, but I didn't let on. I did wonder why we didn't have a better car and better house being he had such a smart brain. My mother must have been thinking more or less the same thing because she said, "It's not always about IQ it's about using what we have."

All of a sudden, in my mind's eye, I was back at the library looking at that laurel wreath and all those carvings when I heard my mother say, "Who wants to go first?"

"I'll go first," Carole called.

Bootsie called second.

"I'll go last," my father said, checking my mother's face for a reaction.

"Thank you," she smiled.

My father smiled back but his eyes didn't match his smile. They were dark and brooding. It was like looking at a volcano right before it erupted. Soon his body began to tremble with a slow anger that seemed to build from his feet up. I glanced at Bootsie and she glanced at me and that was it. One second my mother was calling out a word and the next second my father was shoving the Scrabble board across the table and letters were flying everywhere.

"Don't tell me you didn't notice that."

My mother shook her head, exasperated. "What now?"

"You know damn well what I'm talking about. Take off your rose-colored glasses and maybe you'll see what the rest of us see."

"You're talking in riddles," my mother said, putting the Scrabble board back in the box. "When are you going to accept that Betsy was not the reason I got sick. And certainly not the reason your mother got sick."

All of a sudden I realized that my father's mother was sick or had been sick and he wrapped her sickness with my mother's sickness and somehow I was to blame for both of them. None of it made any sense. But mostly I felt bad for my mother, seeing how, once again, my father had stolen the joy right out from under her. Scrabble letters were scattered everywhere. I wanted to help pick them up, but I knew that anything I said or did my father would twist to his advantage. So I kept my mouth closed and my feet still.

A moment later I was sent upstairs. "Your father and I need to talk," was how my mother put it.

"Us too?" Bootsie asked, glancing at Carole.

"No," my father growled and his eyes were the eyes of a madman.

"Good night," I mumbled, and rushed upstairs.

My bedroom was dark, but I didn't turn on a light. I changed into my nightgown and got into bed. Sissy Jupe's tail twitched back and forth against my leg in an effort to settle itself down. Then, out of the quiet, I heard my father yell out a word. They were playing Scrabble without me. I wiped the sweat off of my face and Sissy Jupe climbed onto my chest and stroked my face with his paw.

I closed my eyes for the longest time, but I couldn't sleep.

"Are you awake?" It was Bootsie's voice.

I opened my eyes and the black air slowly parted and my mother's fake moon and stars shined down at me. They looked so bright that, for a brief moment, I began to name them. "B-i-g D-i-p-p-e-r, L-i-t-t-l-e D-i-p-p-e-r." But my brain knew they weren't real. It didn't matter; I ran out of names. I didn't know much about stars.

"Can you hear me?"

"No," I groaned, and closed my eyes and I kept them closed until morning.

It was almost noon when I was on the porch step and Bootsie put a cookie on Sissy Jupe's head, laughing. I wondered if she had gone bonkers, all of a sudden.

"Go away," I yelled, slapping the cookie into the air.

She tried to catch it, but I was too quick. I clenched my fist until the cookie wasn't a cookie anymore, just bits of flour and sugar I poured onto the ground.

"Last time I'll ever spend my money to buy you . . ."

Jean Ann appeared from the side of the house wearing red shorts and a red halter-top, whistling. I took a piece of paper out of my pocket and packed it into a ball. Then I waited until she was close and took aim. The ball almost hit her in the nose, but she stepped sideways just in the nick of time.

"Missed," she yelled, in a smart-aleck tone of voice.

Bootsie laughed, but I gave her a look to shut her up. Of course, Jean Ann took full advantage of the situation. She talked and talked about a whole lot of stuff that wasn't worth remembering, so I didn't. It was Bootsie who finally managed to stop pouting long enough to say, "Anyone ever say you talk too much?"

"No, but you do."

"Does not." I flashed my eyes at Jean Ann when I said it. She opened her mouth to speak but no words got out. It was just as well because I could tell by the grin on Bootsie's face that she was sufficiently recovered to give Jean Ann a good tongue-lashing. I would've egged Bootsie on, but my father was due home and I needed to get going.

"Anyone for Shop-Rite?" I tossed the question into the air, but it was Jean Ann who took hold of it.

"I'll go," she said.

"Are you coming?"

Bootsie thought it over for a minute before she answered. "Nah, but they got free fresh-squeezed orange juice. I saw the sign yesterday in the window."

Well the thought of getting free orange juice made me forget all about my father for a moment. I pictured myself standing in line, with men wearing ties and women pushing grocery carts in front and back of me, looking grown-up.

"Let's go," I said, grabbing Jean Ann by the arm.

When we got to Shop-Rite, we checked the front window and in between a sign for canned peas and a sign for Wheaties, somebody wrote: "Free. Fresh-squeezed orange juice. Fri. noon to three."

We went inside and read the clock on the back wall. It was eleven-forty-five.

"Let's check out the lipstick and nail-polish," Jean Ann said.

Well, after we got done rolling up about a thousand lipsticks, we started in on the nail polish. We picked up the bottles by their necks and shook them real good so we could watch the color fold into itself. When we were done, we matched-up nail polish with lipstick and decided what we would buy if we had the money to buy anything. I stashed my selections—a tube of Flaming Ice lipstick and a bottle of Red Tango nail polish—behind a rack of nail clippers.

"What are you doing?"

"I might come back later and buy one."

Jean Ann looked at me as if I was crazy. "They cost fifty-nine cents apiece."

"I said, 'Might,'" and adjusted the rack to make sure my lipstick and nail polish were one-hundred and five percent hidden.

"I'm thirsty," Jean Ann said, and walked away.

The orange juice line was just as I had imagined it. Everybody in line was grown-up, except Jean Ann and me. I pulled my shoulders back and held my chin up so I would look a little taller. Jean Ann did the same. When we got to the front of the line, a pretty lady in a white dress with a ruffled orange-colored apron handed us two cups and said: "My you girls look thirsty." We drank the juice straight down without coming up for air and handed her our empty cups. It was great fun.

On the way home Jean Ann and I decided to come up with a plan to get more free orange juice. It took some thinking. We finally agreed to go home and throw ourselves down the stairs and break our arms, then go back to the store with our arms in slings. We reasoned that two broken arms would get us a ton of orange juice if we wanted it.

"See you soon," I said, and we made a solemn oath to break our arms and meet in an hour. Jean Ann ran inside her house and came right back out. "It's twelve-thirty," she said. Then we parted.

My mother and Carole were hanging out wash and Bootsie wasn't anywhere around when I stood in the hall, studying my situation. I have to admit that throwing myself down a flight of stairs was a lot harder to do than I had imagined. I mean looking straight down fourteen wood steps almost made me want to go back on my word. But I knew I would never be able to live with myself if I chickened out. In the back of my head, I kept seeing Jean Ann hurling herself down the stairs outside of her bedroom and I knew what I had to do. It didn't seem fair that her stairs were carpeted and there were only nine of them, but I told myself it wasn't her fault that her parents had laid carpet all over the house.

I shoved Jean Ann out of my head and took a deep breath to calm my jitters. Then my eyes went down the stairs, slowly, one at a time, just like feet do when they aren't in too much of a hurry. It took me about ten or twelve false starts, but I finally got my courage up and leaned forward until I felt my feet raise up and my body shoot down the stairs and land in a heap in front of the clothes hamper.

For a minute, I just laid there, dazed. I didn't know if I was dead or crippled or what. My whole body ached. Slowly, I tried to stand up. I rested most of my weight against the wall, and straightened one leg, then the other. Next, I tried working my arms. My right one moved all right but the left one had a big bruise on it and the elbow was bent and it hurt when I tried to straighten it. But I reasoned it wasn't broke because my good arm showed it how to move, and it did. I knew Jean Ann would gloat over the fact that she had a real broken arm and I didn't. For a moment I thought about trying again, but I decided that I had had all the pain for one day I could stand. So I got a cotton scarf out of the hall closet and folded it into a sling. Then I swung the sling over my head and set my arm down gently, and waited.

Just like clockwork, Jean Ann showed up at one-thirty wearing a flowered scarf folded and knotted at her neck just like mine. Only her sling was made out of silk and it kept sliding up her arm and she had to keep fooling with it so her arm didn't fall out. I sensed something was wrong.

"Let me see," I said, stepping closer.

Jean Ann jumped back and hollered, 'No' so fast you would've thought I'd asked her to walk on hot coals.

"You didn't break your arm," I sneered. "You're faking."

I threw in the last part to round out my suspicion, and then I waited for her response. It wasn't long in coming.

"My mother was home," she said, dropping her eyes. "Besides, nobody'll know the truth."

Jean Ann's words buzzed around in my head, and the more they buzzed, the more I realized that she was missing the point: we gave our word.

After that, my estimation of Jean Ann went from bad to worse. I reasoned that anyone who would break a solemn oath about something as serious as breaking your arm was beyond hope. So I said, "Forget it," and we started walking. A moment or so later she said, "Let me see *your* arm."

I stopped dead in my tracks. Jean Ann was accusing me of being as chicken-livered as she was. That was more than I could take. I slid my arm out of my sling. "How do you think I got this giant bruise?"

Her eyes were as big as saucers.

"I . . . I tried," she stammered. "But you know how my mother is about me getting hurt."

I slid my arm back into the sling and shook my head.

"Forget it," I repeated. "Pretend."

"I can do that," she said, adjusting her knot.

I thought it over for a minute, then I added: "If the juice lady says anything just moan when she hands you the cup and you should be all right."

Jean Ann nodded her approval. Then we walked back to Shop-Rite with slings on our arms and thoughts of free orange juice in our heads.

The orange juice line was about a mile long, so we decided to pay another visit to the lipstick and nail polish aisle. Jean Ann picked up a hairbrush with a handle that folded over the bristles when you aren't using it, and brushed her hair.

"Stop that nobody wants your cooties."

She pulled strands of her hair out of the bristles and blew them into the air, laughing.

I rolled my eyes and moved aside a handful of nail clippers to see if my polish and lipstick were still where I had stashed them. They were there all right, so I put the nail clippers back just so. Jean Ann was brushing her hair.

A woman carrying a small baby frowned at Jean Ann and she hung the brush back on the rack.

"Ouch," she moaned, fooling with her sling. "My arm is killing me."

I could feel the woman's eyes watching us as we walked away. "Let's forget the orange juice," Jean Ann suggested.

"No," I said, and lifted my bad arm to drive home my point.

"What if she tells the manager?" Jean Ann pleaded.

"Can't say I didn't warn you."

Well that day I learned no matter how careful you are, whenever you do something the second time around it's never as exciting as it was the first time. Take the orange juice. The orange juice lady was real nice and we managed to look sufficiently wounded and all, but something was missing.

"My, oh my," she said, when it was our turn. "Careful with those arms."

Jean Ann let out a little moan and glanced at me out of the corner of her eye. I signaled for her to speak. "Thank you," she said, sniveling.

The lady smiled real wide and handed us two cups. The juice tasted good. But the truth is I couldn't wait to get out of there.

When we were in full view of her house Jean Ann took off her sling and wrapped it around her wrist like a bracelet.

"We fooled her," she bragged.

I didn't say anything.

Jean Ann paused before she tapped my good arm.

"How come you left that woman you used to live with?

Her question caught me by surprise. I slid my sling off and tried to straighten my arm but it wouldn't straighten so I put the sling back on.

"For me to know and for you to find out."

"I had fun," Jean Ann said, and ran up her driveway with both arms swinging wildly at her sides.

"Howdy." I glanced up and saw Woody smiling at me. He was in his truck.

"Hi." I tried my best to sound cheerful when I said it.

"I put three empty cases of soda bottles under the porch for you." Woody's good eye was on my sling. "Need help getting them just holler."

"Thank you," I whispered, and hung my head because genuine kindness can really do a number on you if you aren't expecting it.

"You're welcome, neighbor." I felt Woody's huge leathery hand on the top of my head, and then he drove off.

XI

Old Gray Nose

I watched Woody's truck pull in front of his house and park. For a long moment he sat there with his hand out the window. Finally, he threw what was left of his cigarette on the street and walked inside.

I scraped my flip-flop on a rock until a wad of gum fell off. Then I straightened the cardboard sole I had cut and rubber-cemented over a hole, stamped a few times to keep it in place, and kept walking.

It was late July and Mrs. Benson was weeding her garden to give her newly planted petunias more sun. Out of the corner of my eye, I saw a brown dog with a long gray nose and short, skinny legs crossing the street towards me. I lowered my head and pretended I didn't see him, but, of course, I did. Anyway, when the dog got closer I noticed he was wearing a collar but no tag so I thought he might have a home and he might not. I patted the top of his head and the dog looked up. I could see in his eyes that he liked me a whole lot. All of a sudden I realized I was crying so I slid the sling off of my arm and dried my eyes.

"You lost?"

I continued up the street and the dog did his best to keep up. We passed a Mister Softee and turned onto Jackson Avenue and kept going. In front of Butchie Boswell's house, we saw a man climbing to the top of a telephone pole. The man was wearing a tool belt with about a thousand tools on it, and the weight of all those tools pulled his trousers down and made the crack of his hiney show. His hiney had to be hot staring at the sun. But if the man noticed, he didn't let on. He kept climbing and the higher up he got, the lower his trousers got. If I had been in a better mood, I would have laughed. Instead, I straightened the cardboard again, and I felt the dog lick my leg, and when he was done he sat on his haunches and let out a few tired-sounding grunts.

I reached out my good arm and scratched his head. "You'll be okay."

A car was coming up fast behind us so I looked around. Elvis Presley was on the radio and Boy Boy had the volume turned way up. I plugged my ears with my fingers.

Boy Boy pulled alongside of us and revved the engine a few times.

"Nice mutt," he snickered, and rounded the corner on two wheels.

"Creep." The word was no sooner out of my mouth when my mood brightened considerably. I secretly thanked Boy Boy for taking my mind off of being one place and wanting to be another.

"What's your name? Rover? ... too common ... Buddy? ... no ... Old Gray Nose? Yes. Hello, I'm Running Fawn.

Welcome to The Daughters of Pocahontas."

I lifted Old Gray Nose's chin and checked his eyes for a reaction. His eyes were all bright and shiny so I knew he liked his new name just fine.

"C'mon," I said, yanking his collar to get his legs moving. We rounded the corner, where we saw Sarah and Jean Ann lining up at the Mister Softee window.

"Who's that?" Sarah's tone said mutt, not cool.

"My dog," I replied, and picked up the pace.

"Is not," Jean Ann yelled. Old Gray Nose took off running and I took off after him.

When he got to Woody's lot he stopped to pee.

"All done ... come on," I begged, and motioned for him to follow me across the street and into the crawl-space under the porch. "Don't worry, Delaware doesn't have bad spiders. Mama Cope says they all live in Texas."

I paused to see if he was listening, and he was. All of a sudden, a car horn sounded and I ducked behind a hedge.

"No!" As I spoke I felt Old Gray Nose rub his wet nose against my leg. "Not you boy," I said, and peeked around the hedge to get a better look. The horn sounded like my father's horn, but the car was yellow. A moment later I heard another car horn and this time I knew it was my father's car by how hard it took the potholes. I couldn't see his face, but I saw him get out of the car and put a white bag in his overalls. Then he went in the house and I tiptoed out from behind the hedge and lifted the door to the crawl-space under the porch, slowly. The door had loose slats with pieces of wood missing. I had to be extra careful they didn't bang into each other and give Old Gray Nose and me away.

I had to yank on Old Gray Nose's collar to get him to come into the crawl-space with me, but he did. Then I let the door down inch by inch.

It wasn't real dark, but it took my eyes a minute to adjust. Every once in a while the sun streamed through the door and formed what looked like a large tic-tac-toe puzzle on the dirt floor. The puzzle had pieces missing that matched the slats in the door.

Old Gray Nose barked.

I nearly fell on him trying to shut him up. "Sssshhhh."

Overhead there were wood beams with sharp nails sticking out of them, so I hunched over to avoid getting stabbed. The fattest beam marked where our house ended and Woody's house began. Here the ground widened to make way for the porch. Of course, I couldn't see the part that people walked on because I was looking up, not down.

"They're here someplace." I got on all fours and crawled closer to the steps. My eyes mowed every inch of that dirt. Against the far wall was a bicycle with no seat; a cobweb with two shiny spiders, and a rusty shovel painted red. Everything else was dirt; I kept crawling. That's when I saw them. Under the lowest step were Woody's soda bottles. Three whole cases.

"Bingo!" I said, dragging them into the open. The cases were made of wood and covered with a loose layer of dirt. I went into a coughing fit I muffled with my hand. "Let me see seventy-two bottles at two cents apiece is . . . um ... one dollar and forty four cents . . . ."

After I had tallied my take, I took off my sling and wiped one of the bottles clean. The sling worked, but my arm ached something awful.

I was resting my arm when I saw the access door lift up and a stream of sunlight sneak in. I put the bottle back and leaned sideways to block the cases from view. Then the door dropped down and the light faded.

Old Gray Nose barked.

"Who's under there?" It was my father's voice.

I didn't say anything. I watched the door lift up again. I squinted to adjust to the brightness, and then I opened my eyes wide. That's when I saw a pair of overalls coming towards me and I started shaking and couldn't stop. Oh no, I mouthed, and my good arm pushed the cases behind me.

"Bugs, that you?" I couldn't have said anything if I had wanted to, and I didn't want to because I was afraid.

Old Gray Nose barked.

"Where'd the dog come from?" My father's eyes had a scary look in them. "Answer me."

"I found him."

"Is that right... do you know what time it is?"

"No."

"No, what?"

"No, Daddy."

"Dinner time." My father's loud voice set off more barking.

"He won't bite, he just likes to bark."

My father extended his hand and let Old Gray Nose have a good sniff.

"Expensive collar. No tag, but he belongs to somebody."

"Can I keep him?"

"Get in the goddamn house." My insides were shaking, but I was too stubborn to give up.

"I'll take good care of him."

"I'm sure."

When he put it like that I decided to dig deeper. "He's a great watch dog."

My father shook his head. "After all the trouble you caused, tell me why I should say, yes." And, with that I stepped into the shadows.

Old Gray Nose had another idea. He folded his legs under him. I watched his eyelids roll down slowly. I knew he was about as close to sleep as he could get, without snoring. I could feel my hands shaking as I lifted his chin off of my foot and a sharp pain shot up my arm. I yanked on his collar and he stood up and shook himself good. Then he followed me outside and my father let the door down after us. I kicked a loose slat and then I jerked sideways as if the door had suddenly gone on the attack.

"There you go hurting yourself again." As my father spoke, he took the white bag out of his overalls and handed it to me.

Inside were about a hundred chocolate Kisses. I was about to eat one, when, all of a sudden, I got to thinking about my Mickey Mantle bat and how easy it is to confuse love with hate when you *really* want something, and I handed the bag back to my father.

"Bill, what are you doing? It's time for dinner." My mother was on the porch wiping her hands on a tea towel.

"We need to find who this dog belongs to."

"Can't that wait?" My mother sounded annoyed, but I knew my father would say, no, and we would be on our way, which was exactly what happened.

I started to get in the back with Old Gray Nose, but my father ordered me to sit up front.

At a red light he put the white bag on my lap. "For you." His voice was soft and I would have liked hearing it if it wasn't his voice, the one he used right before he was about to do something awful.

"Good dog." I turned my attention to Old Gray Nose. He was staring out the window like he didn't want to miss anything. A few blocks from Caesar Rodney, my father turned north, so I knew he was headed towards the Weldins'. Of course, I wanted to ask why, but the look on my father's face told me he might say something I didn't want to hear, so I stared out the window, voiceless.

When we got to the Weldins' my father parked next to the trolley barn. "Out ... the dog, too."

Aunt Mary was outside watering her flowers. "What a nice surprise. I just made rhubarb pie. Hot out of the oven."

As we walked a breeze lifted her hair just enough for me to see bruises on her neck shaped like fingers. This made me look closer and that's when I noticed there were more bruises on her legs and one on her arm.

"Welcome." She patted Old Gray Nose on the head as she spoke.

Suddenly, I heard a howl. Spot was standing on his doghouse, watching.

"He isn't used to being around other dogs," Aunt Mary said, holding the screen door open. "Better bring your dog inside."

The inside of the house was shaped like the inside of the Bensons' garage only it had rooms. The kitchen had a table and four chairs, the smallest refrigerator I had ever seen, a potbelly stove, and a sink with no spigot for water. Behind the stove were two more rooms. Each room had a small bed and a small dresser, nothing more.

As we were eating our pie, which was cooked just right and topped with vanilla ice cream, the door opened.

"Frank ... Tommy. We have company. This here's Betsy, Bill's youngest."

Uncle Frank glanced at his wife, then me. "Pleasure," he said, reaching for a plate with a slice of pie on it. He was as tiny as Aunt Mary, but he pulled his shoulders back when he walked, which made him appear much taller.

"About time I get to meet you." He looked me in the eye when he said it. I was expecting my father's eyes—the kind that can make a person hide in fear of what *might* happen. But once again I was reminded that what we expect isn't always what we get. There was a deep sadness in Unkle Frank's eyes, which he seemed aware of in a turn of the head sort of way.

Without warning, my father pounded his fist on the table and the plates and silverware rattled. Tommy opened his mouth to speak, but Uncle Frank beat him to it. "We're eating," he said, but his tone said a lot more. It said: You're in my house. Don't ever do that again.

Aunt Mary took my father's empty plate off the table and put it in a rubber pail in the sink. "Can I get you anything else?" She was real gracious, but I could tell by her mood that the sooner my father was out the door, the happier she would be.

"I was wondering if you wanted another dog."

Aunt Mary looked at my father and then she looked at me and repeated what she had said earlier, "Spot isn't used to being around other dogs."

"Always a first time."

Uncle Frank shook his head and said, "The answer is, no."

For most of the way home my father stared out the windshield as if he were reading a map in his head and couldn't decide which line went where.

When we drove past Caesar Rodney and onto Brighton Avenue, I felt an explosion of thankfulness. A moment later, my father rubbed my thigh and said, "How badly do you want that dog?"

I pushed myself closer to the passenger door to get as much distance between us as possible. My father took a pothole extra hard and pulled in front of the house. "I tried. Now get the hell out."

My mother was on the porch. "I see you still got the dog . . . where have you been?"

"Frank's," my father said, pushing Old Gray Nose inside the house.

"What . . . they can't even afford to feed themselves, let alone another dog. Go wash up for dinner."

I peed a long time because I had been holding it in rather than risk getting stuck in some smelly outhouse.

"B-e-t-s-y."

I went downstairs and sat at the table. A few moments later, my father and Old Gray Nose showed up. Carole's eyes nearly fell out of her head. Bootsie must have been surprised, too, but she held onto her feelings real good. I discovered why when she opened her mouth to speak.

"What are we going to name him?" she said, getting right to the point.

"Where'd he come from?" Carole aimed her accusing eyes at me as she spoke. "Somebody's yard?"

"No, he was . . ." I began, but my father finished. "Lost."

I could hardly believe my ears. My father was taking up for me. Suddenly, I was confused for good.

"Carole, listen to yourself. You're getting too old to tattle-tale."

As my mother spoke my father gave Old Gray Nose a ham bone and I watched the dog eat all the meat off of it and chew on the bone. When he was done, he folded his legs under him and fell sound asleep. He snored, too.

"Better keep Sissy Jupe upstairs," my mother frowned. "The dog would probably scare him half to death."

I patted Old Gray Nose on the top of his head and winced in pain. My father and mother were watching, but neither one said anything.

"You may be excused," my mother said, and I went upstairs. Sissy Jupe was sitting in our bedroom window.

"I got you something," I said, feeding him pieces of ham.

Moments later my mother entered the room and stood at the foot of my bed. "Want to tell me what happened?"

"I found him . . . ."

"I'm not talking about the dog. I'm talking about your arm."

I tried to straighten it but it hurt too bad. I looked at my mother and she looked at me and the next thing I knew my voice was coming at me and her eyebrows were raised and she said, "Fell? How did you manage to do that?"

That's right. I said I fell. I didn't plan to, but that's what came out.

"Just tell me the truth, what happened?"

"I . . . tripped."

I could tell by my mother's expression that she didn't believe me. But instead of questioning me to death like my father always did, she combed my hair away from my forehead with her fingers and said, "You need to be more careful, you could've really hurt yourself."

Her voice was so soothing I was tempted to spill my guts. But her eyes looked tired and it was obvious to me that she had enough problems, without adding mine to her load.

"Don't forget to give Sissy Jupe water, and keep your door closed." Then she left.

I fed Sissy Jupe the rest of the ham and filled his water bowl. That's when I heard somebody step onto the porch and the front door open. I went to the window, but I couldn't see who was talking because the porch roof was blocking my view. The first voice I heard was my father's.

"Might be," he was saying.

"His name is Max," a woman's voice replied. "We live around the corner on Jackson. My neighbor thought she might have seen Max with your daughter."

I chewed on my lip and listened some more.

"She found him wandering on the highway near the Vet Hospital," my father lied. "Let me go get him . . . assuming, of course, we're talking about the same dog."

It got real quiet for a minute or two, and then the woman's voice came at me again.

"You had me worried half to death. Get over here, boy."

I heard footsteps again, and then I heard the woman fooling with a pocketbook or something.

"Here, please give this to your daughter and thank her for me."

"I sure will."

"C'mon Max, time to go home."

A few moments later I saw the woman, she had short hair and glasses, walk up the street with Old Gray Nose and disappear.

"My dog," I said, wrapping my good arm around Sissy Jupe and kissing his big orange head. "I named him."

XII

Meteor

It was a hot August evening with mosquitos circling streetlights and crickets chirping to a starless sky. I slid the glider closer to the porch railing and fanned myself with a piece of cardboard from an empty Cheerios box. Behind me, I could hear Mrs. Hicks start up the record player and a man with a high-pitched voice singing something about wanting Jesus to save him and Mrs. Hicks singing the same thing, only louder. Their voices poured out of her half-open door onto the street where Woody's truck was parked next to the curb, and Woody, with a cigarette hanging from his lip, waved.

I waved back, and just as I did, Boy Boy's Chevy appeared over the rise doing about one hundred miles an hour. At first I couldn't see Boy Boy, but I could hear his radio the whole way. It was loud but Mrs. Hicks was louder. "Save me my sweet Jesus . . . ."

Woody hit his horn a few times, a harsh, bullfrog

sounding horn that cut into the starless sky, and overpowered Boy Boy's radio. Boy Boy didn't seem to notice. The only thing that finally slowed him up was the fact that he was running out of street. By the time he got to the Bensons', his car went into a skid and he almost hit a girl on roller skates before regaining control and pulling alongside Woody.

Woody shook his fist and the two of them got into a heated conversation, which included a lot of swearing and head shaking. Finally, Boy Boy gassed his engine five or six times, as if to make sure he had the last word and took off up the street, honking.

My father opened the screen door. "What the . . ." Then he saw Woody and stopped mid-sentence.

Woody passed me a wink with his good eye and disappeared into his house.

"What's going on?" My father knocked the bowl of his pipe on the railing as he talked. Tiny bits of burnt tobacco rained onto the porch. When he was sure it was empty, he stuck the pipe into his pocket, bowl first.

"Take me home sweet Jesus, take me home . . . ."

My eyes started watering. Take me home, I sang, without moving my lips.

"Goddammit." My father leaned over the edge of the porch and pointed his eyes straight up. I pointed my eyes in the same direction, but I couldn't find what he was after. The only thing I saw was a small, yellow sliver of moon sitting above a patch of clouds.

"Newspaper promised a meteor and damn if they didn't screw up again." As he talked the bib of his overalls strained to cover his bare chest, so when his arms moved, the bib didn't.

"A real meteor?" My voice sounded surprised because I

was.

"Should've been here by now." My father was talking but his eyes were on his watch. "Can't believe a thing people say anymore."

I waved my cardboard fan faster. "Place is a damn swamp." My father scratched his temple where a mosquito had left a large, red welt. "Breed malaria . . . tried to tell them." My father's voice faded in and out as if he were having a private conversation with himself and I just happened to be there to witness it.

In the background, I could hear Mrs. Hicks and the man on the radio still screaming at Jesus. Then I heard a door slam and the screaming stopped.

I looked around and everywhere I looked, the air was getting grayer and grayer.

My father smacked his hand on his arm and smashed a mosquito. "Inside," he said. "For once you're going to do what I say . . . . MOVE."

My body was shaking but my brain was working okay. Careful, it said.

"Daddy," Carole called from the dining room.

"I'm coming," he called back. I took two giant steps to avoid being knuckled in the back and it worked—all I felt was a light push.

"Look!" Carole and Bootsie were holding up wads of newspaper coupons.

"Double coupon night," my mother said, stuffing the coupons into her purse. "Lines'll be a mile long."

"Are we all going?" Bootsie said.

My mother's eyes were blazing. "You know as well as I do the car won't start, so why ask?"

"I meant Betsy."

My mother glanced at my father, before she turned her

eyes on me. "Up to him."

"It doesn't take four people to push one grocery cart," he growled.

"I'll stay . . ." Bootsie began, but my mother cut her short. "Enough chitter chatter. We need to get going."

Bootsie drummed her fingers on the table and signed: fast.

"What are you two up to . . ."

"Bill, quit while you're ahead," my mother warned.

"I just don't want them taking advantage of you."

My mother responded by pointing at a metal grocery cart leaning against the wall. "I said, 'We need to get going.'"

"Hup, two, three, four," Bootsie said, pushing the cart out the door behind my mother and Carole.

For a minute or two I could hear them talking, then everything got real quiet. I looked around. The room was lit with one small, clay lamp that sent its brightness straight up. On the ceiling above the lamp, a full white moon glowed. It was as if the light gave the room a life of its own. It wasn't a real moon. But I couldn't take my eyes off of it.

"You enjoy staring at the ceiling?" My father was standing in front of the television with his arms folded at his waist, grinning.

I couldn't think of a thing to say so I kept my eyes on the ceiling, hoping to put his question to rest. But he kept going.

"They locked my mother away for staring." It was a mean thing to say, and I despised him for saying it.

"Tea?" I don't know how in the world I came to ask about tea, except that I didn't want to hear any more of his mean talk.

"Stop playing games and move."

I was behind him until I got to where the white linoleum in the dining room ended and the brown linoleum in the kitchen began. Behind me a ceiling lamp sent faint rays of light over my shoulders into the kitchen.

"Over here." My father was standing in front of the sink.

The kitchen was as black as asphalt. My eyes took a few seconds to adjust to the darkness. Then they narrowed on my father. He was smiling. I flipped up the switch for the overhead light.

"Off," my father said, his rising voice betraying his fake smile.

"But . . . I . . . I need light . . ."

"Forget the tea." It was the same voice he used when he was up to no good. I tried to move, but my feet stuck to the linoleum as if they were glued.

Suddenly, there was a loud knock on the front door.

"Stay put. I'll be right back."

I waited a few minutes, then my feet freed themselves and tiptoed to the dining room where I hid behind the buffet so I could hear what was going on. Moments later, Boy Boy's voice started drifting my way. From what I was able to glean, Boy Boy was establishing a meteor-selling business and wanted my father to partner with him.

Boy Boy said they would be rich in no time at all. And, he said, if they ran out of meteors, they could sell granite at the same price and no one would know the difference.

"First, you need to find a meteor," my father said.

"It's coming." Boy Boy's voice sounded excited. "Moses said so himself in the Bible."

"Moses did, did he? Your mother tell you that?"

"Yep."

"Ask her where it's landing at and we're in business."

Boy Boy promised to return the following day. Then I

heard my father mumble and Boy Boy laugh and the door close. I ran back in the kitchen just in time.

"Wouldn't know a meteor from a hole in his head." My father lit the pilot light under the teakettle. "Did you miss me?"

My father seemed to get a lot of pleasure out of asking me questions for which the only safe answer was no answer. And this question was no exception.

"Just you and me," he smirked.

My thoughts were running too fast to grab hold of them. I opened the cupboard and reached for the canister of tea bags.

"Here it is."

"Here what is?"

"Tea bags, Daddy," I said, and set the canister on the stove.

"Well, the last I heard *here* means *here*... not over there."

"I... I'm getting a mug."

I had both hands in the drain-board when I felt my father grab hold of my waist and pull me back towards the stove. "Relax," he whispered in my ear.

I glanced over my shoulder at the clock on the wall above the sink. It was eight-thirty.

"They'll be fast."

My father let go of my waist and opened his mouth and laughed so hard his whole body shook. Then he lifted my bangs and kissed my forehead. "Don't worry. Did you see the wad of coupons they had?"

I shook my head, no.

"The games are over." The laugh was gone and there was an anxious drawl in my father's voice. "It's time to grow up and stop acting like a kid."

My father's words made me feel afraid and ashamed at the same time. I tried, but once again I knew there was no right thing to say. He lifted my chin and pressed his lips against mine.

"Mmmm," he crooned.

I covered my mouth with my hand.

My father pushed my hand away and I felt his tongue force its way into my mouth. Again, I tried to cover my mouth and again he stopped me. "Loosen up," he said, and turned off the stove.

I caught my lower lip between my teeth to hold in the tears. I didn't know what my father was up to and I was afraid to find out. I sat the mug on the stove, locking my elbow to maximize the distance between us. Then I lifted the teapot and a spray of steam shot past my nose, upward. I poured the boiling water into a pitcher and added tea bags and sugar. The aroma of fresh-brewed tea quickly filled the room. My hand was shaking but I managed to pour the tea into the mug and added some ice-cubes.

My father watched me, closely.

"Okay, you made your tea."

I glanced at the teapot, steam still rising out of its spout. My father stepped closer; I stepped to the side. I took a deep breath and let it out with a gasp.

"I'm onto you," he snorted, and led me upstairs.

"Please don't."

"Don't what?" he laughed, pulling me into his bedroom. "I haven't done anything."

I wiped my eyes on my shirt and looked around. In one corner was a flowered, upholstered chair with a pair of nylons across its back. Next to the chair was a bed and across from the bed was a dresser. The dresser was made of maple and one of the knobs was missing. On top was a hairbrush and Evening in Paris cologne. I was staring at the cologne when I saw it: a letter in Mama Cope's handwriting. I was determined to get hold of it. A moment later I got my chance and I took it. As my father was walking towards the window, I tossed the letter from behind my back into the hall. It was like a scene out of Nancy Drew. My father didn't see a thing.

"Relax," he said, pulling the window shade down. Suddenly, the room went as dark as Hades.

The bed was covered with a white sheet and had a red blanket hanging over the footboard. The pillows, there were three of them, were half in and half out of wrinkled, white pillowcases.

I strained my eyes to see more. My father unfastened his overalls and pulled them down his thick, hairy legs.

"Feel this," he said, flexing his thigh muscles.

When I didn't move, he hopped closer, and pressed my hand to his thigh.

"Pure muscle."

I took a deep breath and locked my eyes on his, hoping he would see, in my eyes, how much I hated touching him. But he didn't. He kicked his overalls off and forced my hand between his legs.

"I forgot your tea, I'll go get it."

My father responded by forcing my hand to rub him in short, jerky strokes.

"Thata girl." His voice was full of tobacco.

I tried to pull my hand away, but he stopped me. "You're upsetting *him*," he said, lifting my dress over my head.

I lunged for my dress, and missed.

"Have to be a lot quicker than that," he laughed, and pulled my panties down and stuck his finger inside of me.

"O-u-c-h ... please don't. You won't go to Heaven."

"Ahhhhh." His voice sounded strange like he was talking to himself and I wasn't even there. Tears fell out of my eyes and down my cheeks.

"Please stop, *please*."

My father shoved me onto the bed. I tried to reach for my dress again, but he pulled my hand away.

"You have a beautiful body."

I folded my arms across my chest and curled my shoulders, hoping that his conscience would click on and he would stop. Instead, he took his shoes and underwear off. Then he turned towards me and flexed his arms.

"Watch this," he laughed.

I glanced past him to the clock on the wall. It was nine-fifteen.

"They'll be home soon."

"You let me do the worrying."

When he was done talking, he made a little game of untying my shoes by kissing my stomach and humming one of those songs men in the Army sing when they march. "Feel good?" he said, stuffing his tongue into my belly button.

I tried to push him away, but his body didn't budge. "Please stop ... *please*."

"SSShhhh." My father arched his back, dangled his thing close to my face, and laughed. "Aren't you going to say, hello?"

I closed my eyes and tried not to breathe. I read one time that if you hold your breath long enough, your brain won't get enough oxygen and you'll faint. But just when I began to feel a little dizzy, my father shook my bad arm and I started breathing again.

"I'm waiting."

I turned my head, but my father turned it back. "Hold him."

Suddenly, and without warning, I felt something hot and hairy in my hand. It felt like the skin of a newly plucked chicken. "Stop acting like a kid."

When I looked down I saw the ugliest thing I ever saw. It was even uglier than the pictures I saw in the burned-out mansion. My body was trembling.

"You're making him get big," he said, swinging his hips in a fast circle.

"No . . . ." It was my voice, but it sounded sort of mechanical, like a wound-down toy.

My father got on top of me and pushed his thing between my legs. Then he lowered himself, slowly.

"I can't breathe," I heard myself say.

My father pressed harder and harder and low, dry moans came out of his mouth in loud gasps. I felt sweat drip off of his face and chest onto my neck and shoulders. And with each drop of sweat, I felt my fear turning into anger, and I trusted my anger to do the right thing, and it did. Whenever my father moved, my hips moved in the opposite direction, forcing him to reposition himself every few seconds or so.

"Stop fighting me." My father lined himself up again, but my body was ready and threw its weight to the opposite side. It took all the strength I had, being that my father weighed over two hundred pounds and I weighed sixty. But somehow my stubbornness paid off and I managed, by sheer willpower, to keep him from going inside of me.

Then, just when I thought I didn't have an ounce of strength left, I felt something wet run down my leg. "Goddamn it," my father yelled. "I told you to relax."

All of a sudden I recalled what Rita Rosini told me

about how babies are made.

"Did we make a baby?"

My father pushed me off of the bed, "Get the hell in the bathroom and wash up."

I pulled my dress over my head and lowered it over my hips.

Out of the corner of my eye, I saw my father walk towards the nightstand and turn on the radio. He switched from station to station until he heard a news announcer.

"Residents just south of the C&D Canal have reported seeing a small meteor land at approximately nine-thirty this evening."

"Oh hell! We missed it."

At that exact moment I saw something shiny like Elmer's glue stuck to my thigh.

"Yuck," I said, as loud and plain as I could.

My father threw my panties at me and I caught them midair. "I said, 'Get in the bathroom and wash up.'"

In the hall I picked up Mama Cope's letter and slid it down the front of my dress. Then, I walked in the bathroom and locked the door.

XIII

Visitation

August 4, 1960

Dear Mr. and Mrs. Toppin,

I hope this letter finds you well. As for me, a moment does not pass that I am not wondering how Betsy is getting along. While I respect the court's no-contact decision, the thought of another month passing without any news is almost unbearable. I pray you can forgive me for phoning and find it in your hearts to share even the tiniest of news. I have enclosed her Sandy Koufax baseball card, which I found under her bed. I know her pretty face will light up when she sees it.

With God's blessing to you and your family,

Rebecca Cope

"Mine," I whispered, holding Sandy Koufax as if I was holding the key that unlocked the mysteries of the entire universe.

One knock and then two more. "Hurry, they'll be here any minute."

I slid the letter and picture back in the envelope. I waited a few minutes, then I looked through the floor register. My father was walking towards the kitchen. I tiptoed across the hall and put the envelope back on my mother's dresser. Then I climbed into my bed and stared up at the fake moon and stars until I heard the grocery cart wheeled onto the porch and willed myself to sleep.

It was late morning when I finally woke up. No one said a word. It was as if I were invisible or didn't matter, which was the way I felt. I sat in the crawl-space for most of the afternoon.

"I know you're in there." Bootsie was looking between the door slats at me. "C'mon, let's go arrowhead hunting."

I held my breath and didn't move.

"I'm looking right at you."

I lifted the door just as my father pulled Lulu to the curb, yellow flames shooting out from under her hood. Moments later we were in the kitchen filling trashcans and buckets with water and running to the car, where a line brigade was formed.

"Keep 'em coming." My father sounded like a four-star general commanding his troops. As buckets and trashcans of water passed down the line my arms began to ache, but it only made me work harder. For the first time since I arrived, I felt what it was like to be a part of something important.

"Keep 'em coming." My father gave me a warning disguised as a smile, and just like that I knew that nothing had changed. Suddenly, my arm grew heavy and water splashed out of my bucket onto the ground.

"Two hands," he said. "This is the last straw. They won't get away with this. I won't let them." My mother told my father he was talking nonsense. "They ... who?"

"It's a conspiracy. My winning sweepstake ticket is also missing."

My mother shook her head. "What are you talking about?"

He opened his wallet and held up a ticket. "Look for yourself, somebody pulled a switch."

"Always *somebody*," my mother said, walking away. "Maybe somebody'll pay our rent ... it's late."

It was like a ritual the way they argued and I offered up prayers that my father would move to California, where if the second part of my prayer was answered, he would find gold and stay there.

Anyway, when the fire was finally out my father headed to bed and Bootsie and I headed to the woods. As usual I was thinking about going back to Mama Cope where I belonged.

"Wow, it's hot." Bootsie's words jolted me to attention.

"Yeah," I said, wondering if my mood was giving me away.

"I love the woods."

"Ditto," I said, looking past her, not daring to look in her eyes.

We ducked under some low branches. "Check the map," and with that I knew Bootsie was back to being an Indian.

When I didn't comply, she signed the word for Indian. I

kept walking.

"Hard head." As she spoke, I pushed aside some high grasses and the path gradually disappeared.

Soon we came to a long row of pine trees, then a small clearing, where here and there we saw a rabbit run in and out of bushes on both sides of us. The land had been cleared recently by the railroad people who tore out most of the trees and brush to lay down new track. The track ran straight through the flattened land as far as the eye could see, with crossties cut smooth and placed just so, and the sunlight hitting the rails like long golden fingers.

"Race you on the track." Of course this meant me losing, so I said, "And don't cheat."

Bootsie tucked her walking stick under one arm, put one foot on each rail, and smiled.

I positioned my feet on the rails and spread my arms for balance. The rails were hot and made my feet sweat.

Every so often, Bootsie would pause to adjust her footing until I caught up. A blind squirrel would've seen what she was doing, but if she wanted me to think otherwise that was fine with me.

Finally, we got off the rails and she ran towards a small hill dotted with tiger lilies and Black-eyed Susans.

"Slow up," I shouted, sucking in air.

"Almost there," she shouted back, and kept running.

I continued up the hill. A light breeze blew the Black-eyed Susans back and forth like tiny rocking chairs. I pulled the collar of my blouse up and over my face to soak up sweat and drew up alongside her.

When we reached the top of the hill and we were about to go down the other side, I leaned forward to see a large honeysuckle bush that was just coming into view. That's when I caught sight of a hummingbird; its wings were rotating like a tiny propeller, above the honeysuckle.

"Look . . . ." That's all I got out before I felt my foot slip into a hole and turn sideways. The next thing I remember is my face hurting and my bottom lip bleeding.

"Let me . . . help," Bootsie said, her voice shaking.

I could move my foot, but every time I tried to put weight on it my leg crumbled. My eyes welled up with tears.

"I probably broke something because of you."

That got Bootsie to inspect my ankle, but she said it wasn't broke because no bones were sticking out. "Try standing." She slipped her arm around my waist and pulled me to my feet.

I couldn't hold back what I was thinking about and I heard myself say, "Last night you deserted me. You lied."

With her arm still around my waist she lowered her eyes and said, "I tried to hurry them, but Carole kept wandering off."

My knees buckled. "So! You promised you wouldn't be long."

"Sorry," she whispered, and handed me her walking stick.

I put my weight on the stick and followed her down a narrow dirt path that stopped at the edge of a big field.

"Look!" Bootsie was pointing at a line of trees just over the next hill.

When we got to the exact spot, a patch of near-dead grass surrounded by swamp pines and loblollies, I dropped the walking stick and Bootsie wrapped her arms around my waist and lowered me to the ground. My ankle was thick with pain but I didn't let on. I tightened my ponytail and watched Bootsie walk over to the nearest tree and snap off a branch. Then she sat beside me, cleaning off leaves and shaping the ends with a penknife she pulled from her pocket. When she was done, she walked back and moved a heavy rock. "I marked the spot," she said, and started digging into the clay earth.

I turned to get a better look and pain shot up my leg. Suddenly, without warning, I was back to thinking about awful stuff and I knew I had to leave soon, no matter what. I wanted to tell Bootsie this, but she was still digging, and with red clay on her hands and face she looked like a real Indian.

Finally, her arms flew up, and she yelled: "I got one!"

"Let me see," I said, excitedly.

Bootsie put a small dark object in my hand. "Perfect point," she said, tracing her thumb along the edge.

I fisted the arrowhead and pulled back a little so she couldn't grab it. "Mine."

"What…" There was a lot of hesitation in her voice, so I pocketed the arrowhead to finalize everything.

A few moments later she stepped behind the trees and just as quickly, she was back. "Need stones to fill in the hole," she said. "Be right back."

When I was sure she was gone, I took my arrowhead out of my pocket, and as I did, an eerie sensation came over me. Suddenly, I saw a ray of light and it cut through the sky with spears of gold so bright I never saw anything like it. It was as if somebody was holding up a zillion candles, and they were all lit at the same time. I wondered if my imagination was playing "make-believe" without me, so I blinked a few times and each time my eyes were drawn to the light. Then, out of the great light, Jesus appeared. He looked a lot like the picture my mother had in the dining room, only somebody forgot to paint the colors in. I didn't see legs, either.

"I am with you always." That's what Jesus said. But I can't say I saw His lips moving because I didn't. I was in shock. Mama Cope taught me to talk to Jesus but she never told me He might talk back and pay me a visit. I knew for a fact Mrs. Hicks talked to Jesus every day and she never got a visit.

I heard footsteps and turned my head. "What's going on?"

I looked up and Jesus was gone.

"Why's your face glowing?" Bootsie's eyes had question marks in them. I was convinced that seeing Jesus was private and I wasn't supposed to tell anyone about it.

"I don't know what you're talking about."

"Yes, you do."

"Do not."

"Nobody can make their face glow . . . not like that."

"I saw Jesus." I said it. I didn't want to, but I did. I didn't expect her to believe me, but the truth was in her eyes.

"How do you know I'm not lying?"

She shook her head. "I already told you. Nobody can do that . . . you're glowing."

"Do you think Jesus was telling us something?"

"You," she said, helping me to my feet.

In the distance I could hear blackbirds call in the treetops. I stretched my head skyward and pulled in the smell of honeysuckle and let it out slowly.

XIV

The Cliff

I was feeding Sissy Jupe 9-Lives tuna when my mother walked in the kitchen and plopped the newspaper on the table; she shook her head, annoyed. I sensed something awful had happened.

"Aunt Mary's dead." It was the first thing she had said since hours earlier when she had burned the bacon and turned the poached eggs into fryers. And even then, when I had expected a cry of disappointment, or anger, she had only managed to hum a few notes of some Peggy Lee song as if this small effort was all she could spare. "Getting upset won't bring her back."

My mother didn't notice the horror on my face as she spoke, and how much her flat tone appalled me; and how much I wished, just once, we would have a real conversation. Above all, she didn't notice that I resented the way she insisted that talking was her choice and I had no say in it.

I tossed the empty 9-Lives can in the garbage and watched Sissy Jupe settle over his bowl to eat. Then I made my way to the table, where my mother had unfolded the paper and put the local section on top. There, I read: "A Wilmington woman, Mary Toppin, stepped onto a track near Miller Road early this morning and was killed instantly by a B&O train. Her purse containing thirty-six cents was found nearby."

I stared into my mother's eyes and tried to guess what she was thinking, but her eyes had a vacant look that made me shudder.

"What's done is done," she said, rearranging and refolding, so the paper looked unread.

For me, there was nothing done about it. Why, I wondered, would Aunt Mary stand on a railroad track and why would some reporter think he needed to tell the whole world she only had thirty-six cents? I wanted answers, but I knew I wasn't going to get any.

"Going to be another hot one."

I nodded and walked out to the porch. There, I sat on the glider, and pushed as hard as I could, hoping by sheer willpower I would fly off the porch and into the heavens.

"Here you are young lady." Mr. Coen bounded from his truck and onto the porch with a bag of hotdog rolls and a box of donuts, rare treats that told me my mother had settled our bill. I anchored the glider with my feet and counted: eight rolls and eight donuts.

Then I looked at Little Miss Sunshine on the packaging, her blue eyes the color of morning and her hair curled just so, and I remembered how Mama Cope used to curl my hair and say, "You are just too pretty for words." I put the rolls and donuts next to me and pushed the glider again, and this time, I almost flew nose first off the porch, and I would have if my mother hadn't suddenly appeared and taken hold of my arm.

"Whoa, it's too nice a day to sit around and mope," she said, and took the rolls and donuts inside, and returned immediately with my father forcing the door open after her.

"Did you hear your mother?" My father used a take-charge tone that caused my mother to fume. "Go back in. I didn't ask for help and I don't need it." I braced myself for what I knew was coming next: my father let out two short snorts and snatched me to my feet. "There you go again causing trouble." As he spoke, he kicked my ankles with his steel-tipped work boots and my legs buckled. "You might fool your mother, but you don't fool me." His eyes were on my legs as if daring them to hobble.

My mother spread her arms out to her sides like wings and stepped between my father and me. He attempted to lower her arms, but she would have none of it. Her teeth were clenched and she was making a low gurgling sound as if she wanted to scream, but didn't want to involve the neighbors. "Bill, for God's sake let go. She was just a baby."

I was not sure what my mother was referring to, but once again I sensed it had something to do with her almost dying when I was born and Mama Cope trying to adopt me. But the more my mother told him to "let go," the more my father dug in and found ten more reasons to hate me.

"She'll learn," he snorted, and then followed my mother back inside.

"What was that all about?" Bootsie sneaked out of the crawl-space wearing high-top tennis shoes that made her bony legs look even bonier. Pointing at my ankle, she added: "Why's it so red?"

I shrugged, and she took off up the street running. Moments later, she yelled, "I won," but I knew better. It was a one-runner race.

When she realized this, she ran back.

"Okay," she said, "What's up?"

"Me, myself, and I."

"Just tell me."

"Tell you what?"

"What happened?"

"Nothing happened."

"You're lying."

"Am not."

"Are too."

I paused. "I'm leaving," I whispered.

"No, you're not."

"Yes, I am."

"Then I'm coming with you."

Bootsie's response took me by surprise. She was willing to risk everything for me and I could not think of one single thing to say. So we started up the street, her eyes looking to the left and mine to the right, respecting each other's silence.

Near the top of the street we saw Shirley Hayes, and her pet skunk, Flower, was on her shoulder.

"What's that?" Shirley pointed at my ankle, where the skin had gone from dark red to dark purple. I shrugged and pulled my socks higher.

"Want to see a new trick?" And just like that Shirley had forgotten all about me and was telling Flower to play dead and he was falling off her shoulder and lying motionless in her arms.

"Zazaam," she said, and Flower began to move.

Being that Aunt Mary was newly dead I fought the urge to laugh, but when Flower stood on his back legs and then bowed at the waist, Bootsie and I howled.

"Shirl . . . ey."

"My mom says we should be on Ed Sullivan . . . have to go."

"Later," we said, and started back down the street.

My father's car was in front of the house, so we headed to Mrs. Samson's.

"Let's check the magnolia tree.

"Coco must be in her cage," Bootsie said, knocking on Mrs. Samson's kitchen door.

"Cage?"

"Shhhhhhh, I hear footsteps."

"Come in, girls," Mrs. Samson said, opening the door. "You here for Coco?"

The house smelled old and on the walls were magazine covers honoring Franklin Roosevelt and Winston Churchill and a framed newspaper picture of Coco sitting in a policeman's arms, sleeping.

"Darn shame," Mrs. Samson said, pointing to the picture, "Coco has to be locked up because grown people insist on acting like children. What's this world coming to?"

Mrs. Samson led us into the kitchen still talking. "Here," she said, passing Bootsie a banana. "You can feed her, just be careful. She gets nervous being caged."

Bootsie and I held onto a long thin railing as we made our way down into a dark, musty-smelling cellar.

"Watch your step," Mrs. Samson called, and flipped the light switch.

On the floor in a big cage next to the washing machine was Coco. She was squinting just like I imagined that Aunt Mary was squinting in that trolley barn the night Uncle Frank got himself drunk again.

"Don't be scared," I said, squatting next to Coco's cage.

"Shhhhhhh," Bootsie whispered, jabbing me in the arm

with the banana. "Don't be so loud."

"Shush yourself." I grabbed the banana out of her hand and pushed it through the bars. Coco's long black fingers peeled section by section and she took a big bite. "Let's ask if we can take her for a ride on your bike and pretend she's our baby."

"What if she runs away?"

"We'll tie her leash to the handle."

"She might get nervous and bite."

"Party pooper." We watched Coco finish her banana.

"Sunshine," I said, and Coco stuck her arm through the bars and handed the peel to me.

"Did you see that?" I said, excitedly. "She likes me."

"C'mon," Bootsie groaned, "before you get both of us in trouble."

When we were back upstairs Mrs. Samson gave us Kool-Aid and thanked us for coming.

"Coco misses people," she said, with a shake of her head.

"Can we take her outside?" I heard myself say.

A look of horror came onto Mrs. Samson's face. "Heavens no. If she gets loose again they'll take her away and lock her up for good."

I was about to mention that she was already locked up, but Bootsie said, "Thanks for the Kool-Aid," and nudged me towards the door.

When we were far enough away to guarantee our voices wouldn't cut back on us, she added: "You almost ruined it."

As she spoke, I tilted my head skyward. "Do you believe in Heaven?"

"Don't ask stupid questions," she said, and kept walking.

At dinner that night we had hotdogs with sauerkraut and the hotdogs were on rolls, not bread, so everything tasted just right. My father was acting a bit strange, but it was a good sort of strange, without any scary stares or dish throwing, so when my mother announced we had a special dessert and served the donuts on a tray lined with a white cloth napkin, I wondered if she was going to say Aunt Mary wasn't really dead and there was hope for us, after all.

My father was reaching for a donut when I felt his eyes on me and I heard my mother say, "This is how dinner should be every night. None of the rigmarole. Now while I have everyone's attention I want to share some good news. Mr. Benson is inviting Betsy to go with his girls to their place on the Chesapeake."

I thought my ears were playing tricks on me. Mr. Benson and I rarely talked, except to say "Hello," whenever I saw him driving past in his Pontiac wagon with a Confederate flag strapped to the antenna.

"I told him, yes." My mother's eyes stopped short of my father as if his response was not needed or wanted. I didn't know how to respond because one part of me wondered if I was being tricked and another part wondered if the Chesapeake was far away and if the water was any good for swimming.

Carole and Bootsie looked disappointed, and more than a little angry. My mother watched all three of us the way she watched letters form words on a Scrabble board; her mouth opened slightly as if she were about to talk or sneeze, I couldn't tell which.

"Why does *she* get to go?" Carole said, dripping chocolate thick as mud down her chin.

"Wipe your chin and don't talk when you're eating," my mother scolded. "There'll be other opportunities."

Bootsie appeared to be in a trance, as if the word, opportunities, was foreign and she had just heard it for the first time.

I studied my father's face, eager to speak, but it was clear to me that my mother was the one doing all the talking and anything I said might stir the pot one time too many. Besides, I could tell by Bootsie's mood, which was becoming increasing trancelike, that she didn't know, any more than I did, what to make of my parents' sudden switch in behavior.

As I watched the back and forth I feared that my father wouldn't remain quiet for long; he would, more likely, come up with some convoluted reason to stop me from going.

Sure enough the next day I overheard him and my mother arguing, and, once again, I felt in the middle of something I didn't want to be in the middle of. My father's voice was loud and firm. He reminded her that I was trouble since the day I was born, and when she stuck by her decision, he used her own words against her by claiming she was setting a bad example by showing favoritism.

"When I don't go to church you hammer me," he said. "How do you think this looks to the other girls?"

I could tell that my father was hoping for a response, but he didn't get one, so he filled up the empty space with more loud talk about setting a bad example and being lectured to every Sunday, noon to dusk, about the very same thing she was proposing I do, and finally he ended by saying, "You're making a big mistake."

My mother's voice was slow in coming like the voice of a lost child, who knows anything she says won't be of any help. "You're making a mountain out of a molehill. I thought, for just once, you'd stop thinking of the past long enough to support me on this."

"Why should I . . . nothing's changed. I should of put my foot down that day in court."

My mother cleared her throat and suddenly a loud noise roared up from her belly demanding to be heard. "Shoulda, woulda, coulda never settled anything," she said. "How many times do I have to tell you that yesterday is yesterday and today is today?"

Shocked by what I had just heard, I tiptoed outside and made my way to the Benson's. There, Sarah and Jean Ann told me we were going to Rock Hall and it was on the Chesapeake River and we would be there for a whole week without any parents around telling us what to do. I could hardly believe what I was hearing: no parents. And, it got better when they got to the part about us watching Elizabeth Taylor movies all day and eating BLT's spread thick with ranch dressing. The more I heard the worse I felt about Jean Ann loving Monopoly and me always winning. That night in bed, I said one Hail Mary and one Our Father, and then I said one more for Aunt Mary and I was glad I did.

For the next whole week I kept my fingers crossed and did a lot of smiling and floor sweeping to up my chances of going to Rock Hall. My father still searched for any reason to back up his rant about me being trouble, but I could tell that my mother's mind was made up. Days passed without any of my father's usual outbursts. Bootsie remained disappointed, but she seemed resigned to the idea that it was better for me to go to Rock Hall than neither of us. Every evening, when my father got home from work she would unload his car and carry brushes and rollers to the basement, where she soaked them in turpentine and told long-winded stories about hitting homers so deep in the woods they clipped passing trains. I could hear my father's laughter make its way through the floor register to my ears, and I knew that for the time being I was safe.

On the morning of the trip, I was packing my suitcase when Bootsie said, "Whew! If I had to make up one more story, I would be brain-dead for sure." Then she showed me a drawing of a house she said she was going to build for us in the woods. She must have been thinking about Aunt Mary when she drew it because the house looked like Aunt Mary's house, without the trolley barn. I think I nodded my approval, but I didn't say much because I remembered how Mama Cope talked about being adopted and this plan had the same bad smell.

"See you soon," I said, and I hurried outside.

"Hope you have your toothbrush," my mother called.

I nodded, and climbed in the back seat next to Jean Ann. Sarah was sitting up front. Behind me I could hear suitcases being loaded into the rear of the wagon. I turned my head just in time to see my father and Mr. Benson shake hands. "Watch her," my father said.

I feared the worst, and then I heard the tailgate slam shut and we were off. The only thing on my mind from that moment on was getting to Rock Hall and spending a whole week with Sarah and Jean Ann without any parents getting in the way. I did feel guilty that Bootsie would be caring for Sissy Jupe and house building, but I told myself I would be extra nice to her when I returned.

As we pulled onto the highway, we started singing about bottles of beer on the wall and Sarah and Jean Ann kept getting the count wrong, but I didn't mind because with every verse there was more distance between my father and me.

When all but five hundred bottles had fallen off the

wall, Sarah pointed to a sign that read, "Welcome to Maryland."

"Almost there," Mr. Benson added. "Almost."

The last two bottles fell as Mr. Benson was turning down a narrow two-lane road with nothing much around except a few farmhouses every now and then. Gradually, the road widened and there was a Texaco gas station with neon red letters that read: "Bait and Tackle." An old black man in rubber fishing boots waved at Mr. Benson and he waved back, with the Confederate flag strapped to the antenna staring down the both of them.

As we continued down the road, no one spoke but I sensed we were almost there and we were. With a few quick turns we were pulling in front of a blue house with a Welcome flag next to the door. Beyond the house was a cliff. I could hear water, but I couldn't see it.

"We're here," Mr. Benson said, killing the engine.

"I got the big bed." Jean Ann opened the passenger door and ran towards the house.

Sarah and I stayed behind to help unload the car.

Inside the house was a ceiling lamp made from the wheel of a real covered wagon. There was a sofa, too, and a chair. I didn't notice anything else because I was carrying in suitcases and groceries, and before I knew it, Mr. Benson was telling us to call if we needed anything, and waving good-bye.

"Thank you," I said, and as soon as he was gone, I ran around the house to see what was what. There were two bedrooms. One had a double bed and Jean Ann had her suitcase on it: the other bedroom had two singles.

"I got the window bed," Sarah said, as if I cared. My mind was on the cliff. Jean Ann said you could see the other side of the world from it. I knew it wasn't true, but from the sound of the water I knew the cliff was steep and the river was wide. I wondered if I swam long enough the river would take me to the ocean, then, once I was declared good and dead from the world, I reasoned it would be safe to return home to Mama Cope and we would be happy.

Later that day I waited for the hush of the land to give way to the power of the river. Still, I couldn't hear the slap-slap of water on shore, so I climbed down the cliff, holding onto its treed sides, too stubborn to turn back. Finally, I stood on the gravelly bottom and pocketed a small red stone. The cold tide washed over my feet. I had misjudged the river's depth and speed. My mind swam for comfort in the image of my newly found stone skimming the river and then riding its current to wherever it was going.

I thought a lot about the river after that. I routinely gave up my Get Out of Jail card and let Jean Ann buy Boardwalk at discount. Sarah swore we were cheating, but I had never known much in life that was fair and square. Gradually, we gave up Monopoly. Instead, we watched Marilyn Monroe movies and ate BLT's on toast so the flavors mixed just so. In the evening we played badminton with two boys who lived in a nearby cottage. Their parents were friends with Mr. and Mrs. Benson. Every day they asked us if we were okay and we always said, yes, with the biggest smiles possible. We knew they were checking on us, but we were grateful they were casual about it and didn't come knocking on our door and making pests of themselves.

Then, exactly one week after we had arrived, Mr. Benson pulled his Pontiac wagon up to the cottage and Sarah yelled, "Time to go home."

With my suitcase in one hand and my lucky red stone in the other, I glanced towards the cliff and took a deep breath, wondering if Bootsie had built us a real house and fed Sissy Jupe twice a day like she promised.

XV

Time to Go

Nobody was home when my mother moved her bedroom dresser downstairs next to the sofa. She had sent Carole and me to Tull's to buy aspirin and Bootsie had gone off with my father, painting. I suppose my mother planned it that way. I never saw her lift anything heavier than a ten-pound sack of potatoes without effort, so how she got a four-foot tall dresser down fourteen steps to its destination was baffling. But somehow she had managed, and by the time we all got home, the dresser was exactly where she wanted it. Her rose-colored hairbrush and Evening in Paris cologne were there, too, on her mirrored tray as casual as anything.

"God damn you." My father was pointing at the dresser, but his eyes were on me. I sank my fingers into the side of the sofa waiting to hear my latest offense. This time it was in his eyes. He was blaming me for the move. I started towards the hall, but he grabbed my arm and turned me around. "You enjoy causing problems, don't you?" His tone was low and watchful—the tone he always used before he erupted. My mind searched for the right answer, but the rest of me knew there wasn't any. "I asked you a question and by God you'll answer."

"Yes."

My father slapped me. "Yes, what?"

He slapped me again. Blood came out of my mouth and down my chin. "I won't let you destroy my family," he snorted, and went for the door.

I waited until I heard his car start up, then I peeked outside to make sure he was gone. I don't remember taking the window screen out, but I do remember screaming, "Liar," and watching blood spray out of my mouth onto the porch.

"What the hell?" Boy Boy was fiddling with his keys and for a split second I thought I saw something resembling human in his eyes, then he snickered and I wiped my bloody mouth with my arm, convinced I hadn't seen anything human after all.

"Stop all that hollering in there."

Suddenly I was aware I wasn't alone in the house. In the kitchen, I could hear the ringer-washer churning clothes into submission. A moment later, I heard my mother singing. "Casey would waltz with a strawberry blonde and the band played on; He'd glide 'cross the floor with the girl he adored and the band played on; But his brain was so loaded it nearly exploded; The poor girl would shake with alarm; He'd ne'er leave the girl with the strawberry curls and the band played on . . . ."

I spit blood on the television. I wanted everyone, especially my mother, who lived inside a songbook to see, with her own eyes, what my father did to me.

"You okay?" Bootsie snuck up behind me and put a cold washcloth across my mouth. I accepted her gesture, even as I was resisting punching her in the head.

"Where were you?"

"Upstairs." She refolded the washcloth with the cool side to my mouth.

I lifted her hand, but she resisted. "It's okay. I'll protect you."

"You said that before."

"This time it's different."

"Too late," I mumbled, pushing her hand away.

Suddenly, I heard the washer stop and my mother and Carole talking. I couldn't hear what they were saying and I didn't care to hear. I tossed Bootsie the bloody washcloth and walked out to the porch. A moment later she was sitting next to me on the glider and we were staring at a squirrel or groundhog, I wasn't sure which, staring back at us. When I saw her mouth open, I hummed, "Yankee Doodle" to cut her off. Then, out of the corner of my eye, I watched her mouth close again and form a tight, thin line.

"Okay, be that way," she said, and stomped inside just as I had hoped. My lip was throbbing from humming and inside my head I kept seeing Aunt Mary standing on that train track, with her pocketbook dangling from her hand, as if she was standing in a grocery check-out line. No, I mouthed, so not a soul could hear, except her.

That night my father didn't show up for dinner again, so my mother ordered us to set the table for four, while, once again, she tried singing her way from ugly to beautiful. "You are my sunshine, my only sunshine. You make me happy when skies are gray . . . ."

After everyone was seated, she focused on her burned chicken and runny potatoes. We knew this was our cue to think about all the starving children in China.

"Be grateful we have food," she said, sprinkling grated cheese on the potatoes.

Carole folded her hands. "I'll say grace."

My mother nodded, yes, but for the slightest second, I thought I detected a no in her yes. Her eyes were on the picture of Jesus.

When Carole was done my mother lowered her eyes and said: "Calcium makes strong bones and teeth."

"When can I take ballet lessons?" Carole whined. "Daddy promised me."

My mother looked up at Jesus again. "Patience is a virtue," she sighed, as if pleading with Jesus to intercede. "School starts in two weeks. We need to go clothes shopping."

She sounded just like June Cleaver with her soft voice that came with a smile. I liked to see her like this, but it was sad, too, seeing how hard she worked at turning ugly into beautiful. "Why don't you make a wish list." As she spoke, she folded her napkin into a tight square. "And remember there are three of you now."

Bootsie gulped her milk and laughed.

"Something funny?" my mother frowned, and with that the wind seemed to go out of her sails and her smile faded.

"Ouch." A piece of burned chicken skin brushed across my busted lip and I felt myself wince. My mother pretended not to notice, but every time she raised her fork her eyes ended up on my face. And behind her eyes there was more. At first I didn't know what. Then, without warning, her words and her eyes caught up with each other and, all at once, became one: *She knows.*

There was still food on my plate when I got up from the table and ran to my room. I expected my mother to stop me, but she kept eating and motioned for Carole and Bootsie to do the same. In my room, I held Sissy Jupe and stared at the fake moon and stars, sorting out bits and pieces of the day, like bits and pieces of an old movie that need to be ordered just so to make any sense.

"You awake?"

I shook my head, no.

"Well, you better be."

I must have fallen asleep without knowing it because I never heard Sissy Jupe clawing a hole in the window screen. I took the screen out and lowered the window.

Outside a quarter moon fell on the street lightly, making everything look a whole lot better than it did in the daylight. I tried to picture what the neighborhood must have looked like when it was new and the street was freshly paved and the houses had shutters and doors painted to match. I imagined it must have been a nice neighborhood then. Women pushing babies in strollers and men standing on their porches, posing, as if they were kings and Jackson Hill was their kingdom. I shook my head and the scene faded.

"You okay?" Bootsie said, yawning.

"Tired."

Hours later, I tiptoed into the hall and out to the porch, looking back every few feet. I was sure that my father or an ax murderer was hiding in the shadows and was going to jump out and grab me at any moment. Slowly, I lifted the door to the crawl-space and a man-sized shadow seemed to move forward right alongside of me.

"Whoa." I tripped over a half-buried root and took a few more steps, this time more slowly. There, in the bare open, not six feet away, my soda bottles were right where I had left them.

I began to drag the bottles towards the door, case by case. With my arm still sore from the orange juice fiasco, I had to stop every few feet and give it a rub. When I finally got to the door, I peeked through the slats and watched a white truck drive past.

"Phew," I said, when I realized I was shaking.

Without making a sound, I lifted the door and dragged the first case to Woody's truck. When I finally got all three cases where I wanted them, I crossed myself, and snuck back inside and went back to bed.

The next morning I got up with the sun. There was a new screen in the window and my bottles were still by Woody's truck, and Woody was standing over them scratching his head.

I tiptoed out the back door and walked around front to avoid waking my mother on the sofa.

"Good morning young lady," Woody said. "Had me stumped for a second, couldn't quite figure out what you were up to."

I stooped to lift one of the cases and a pain shot clear up my arm and nearly paralyzed me. I turned my head but I could feel his good eye watching me.

"Need help?" I waited for the pain to ease up some before answering. "I'm fine," I said, without further explanation. This time it was Woody who paused. He took a drag of his cigarette, then threw what was left in the street and stomped it dead. Finally he said, "How's noon sound for going to Shop-Rite?"

I capped my eyes with my hands as if the sun was bothering me, but the sun was looking the other way.

"Okay," I mumbled, and Woody put the soda bottles in the cab of his truck and drove up the street.

It was about an hour later when my father came home

and went straight to his bedroom and stayed there. My mother gathered Carole, Bootsie, and me into the bathroom and whispered, "Be extra quiet. Your father isn't feeling well."

"Talk to them, not me."

My mother grabbed Carole's arm and shook it. "I'm talking to all three of you. Find something quiet to do."

Bootsie nodded and ran outside, where I found her sitting in one of Woody's junk cars with only one door, and cinderblocks for wheels.

"Don't leave me. Take me with you. I can't go back to the Horners!"

I signed, "Love. Sisters," and her eyes got all watery. I wanted more than anything to make her smile, but I couldn't. I couldn't lie.

So I stared past her to the street and past everything my eyes had ever stared at and I said: "I can't . . . I want to, but I can't . . . I just can't . . . it isn't possible . . . you know that." I tried to stop the words even as they were coming out, but they kept coming. "I have no choice . . . he won't change . . . you're different." Then I turned, took a deep breath, and let the air out slowly.

"When?"

I turned back around. "Tomorrow."

At noon Woody pulled up to the curb. "Howdy girls," he said, and Bootsie and I hopped in. There was a load of garbage in the back, so Bootsie and I held our breath and listened to Woody whistle a Gene Autry song that sounded happy and sad at the same time.

When we got to Shop-Rite, we paused to suck in fresh air and wipe sweat off our faces onto our shirttails. When we caught up with Woody, he was standing in front of a customer service cashier wearing red lips and a smile.

"Let's see," he said, setting the cases on the counter. "Twenty four times three is seventy two bottles if I counted correctly."

The cashier took a dollar bill and some change out of the cash register.

"Belongs to her," Woody smiled, and the cashier counted the change in my hand.

"Thank you," I said, more to Woody than the cashier.

"You girls have a good day," he said, and for a second, I thought I saw his glass eye move. "I have to finish my route."

Bootsie and I ran home, where she emptied the Wampum can onto my bed. "One dollar, two dollars, three dollars, four dollars, five dollars, six dollars . . . ." She paper-clipped the bills, and then counted the change. "Twenty five, fifty, seventy five, one dollar, one dollar fifty, one dollar ninety, two dollars . . . two dollars twenty, two dollars thirty, two dollars forty, two dollars fifty, three dollars, three dollars ten, three dollars twenty five, three dollars thirty, three dollars and thirty cents . . ."

When she was done she put nine dollars and thirty cents in the can and handed the can to me.

"All yours," she said, her voice choking.

"Are you sure?"

"Just promise you won't ever forget me."

"Cross my heart and hope to die." I unpinned Rita Rosini's red ribbon from the hem of my shorts and handed it to her. "It keeps the evil eye away," I said, and she gave me a big hug.

Later that evening my father finally woke up and said, "Everybody in the car. I'm in the mood for something cold."

Lehman's Dairy with its two hundred and eight flavors of ice cream, all homemade and hand-dipped, was about the closest thing to a tourist attraction that Wilmington had and people flocked there by the carload. The thought of eating ice cream was pleasing but experience had taught me that something would go wrong. And it did. Not right away, of course. First, my father had to get his timing just right to make sure he ruined everything all at once.

A girl wearing a cow on her shirt was handing me blackberry ice cream on a sugar cone when my father's voice came at me from behind. He was talking to a man wearing a cowboy hat with a long ostrich feather sticking out of it. The man had nodded his good-bye, but my father was still talking.

"Don't stare," my mother said, so I walked to the car and got in.

"She's dripping," Carole yelled from the front seat.

"Behave," my mother warned as my father opened the driver's door and got in.

"I'm hot."

My mother tapped Carole's arm. "You think you're the only one?"

Bootsie was signing and I followed as best as I could, but with her practicing four hours a day and me not practicing it was hard to keep up.

"What the hell are you two doing?" The next thing I knew my nose was smashed into my father's fist and we were pulling onto the highway.

Carole stretched her arm over the seat and handed me a napkin.

"I'll show you who's boss."

My father pulled over to the shoulder of the road, got out, and ordered Carole to do the same.

"For God sake," my mother pleaded, "get in the car."

"I've heard enough of her baby-ass whining." My father

pushed Carole away from the car and got back in.

"It'll be dark soon," my mother shouted. "She could get run over . . ."

"Can't treat them like children forever," my father said, and drove off.

Out the rear window I could see Carole. She was standing in the middle of the road with the paper ice cream cup in her hand, crying. For a brief moment I forgot all about being scared and I heard myself say, "What about Carole?"

My father swung his fist at me and missed. "You never learn," he hissed. "Do you?"

I nodded my head, instinctively, and my mother said, "Bill, you've made your point."

"Not even close," he said, and pressed harder on the gas.

The sky had turned a dark shade of gray by the time we finally turned around. Carole was standing in the middle of the road where my father had left her. Right there and then I understood what Bootsie must have known all along: my father's approval was temporary and none of us was safe.

"Get in honey," my mother said, and Carole got in. She sat up front as usual, only this time she looked like a mannequin, pale and stiff. My mother kept shaking her head, and Bootsie and I stared at our feet, trying, as best we could, to look like part of the upholstery.

Finally, we turned onto Brighton Avenue. My father hit every pothole. The car bounced up and down like a wild roller coaster and he laughed the whole time.

Then suddenly, without warning, he hit the brake and got out. I tried to see but it was dark and my angle was wrong. "I knew this would happen," he said, and got out of the car.

"What?"

"Jesus Christ," he said, getting back in the car. "When are you people going to start listening to me?"

My mother shook her head. "Will you please just tell us what this is about?"

Again my father didn't answer. We were in front of the house when he ordered everyone out. I was about to open my door, when he said, "Not you . . . you wait here."

I had no idea what was going on when he returned with a shovel and a pillowcase and pulled the car under a streetlight. "Follow me," he ordered.

That's when I saw Sissy Jupe. His eyes and mouth were open and his face was bloody. Tears started down my cheeks and kept coming. I picked him up and pressed his stiff body to mine. "Here," my father said, and eased Sissy Jupe into the pillowcase, gently, as if he were sleeping and my father didn't want to wake him.

"I'd love to know who left the damn door open." My father's voice cracked a little as he spoke. I wanted to say something but once again I was too afraid of saying the wrong thing to say anything.

We buried Sissy Jupe out back under a small dogwood tree. Then my father made a cross out of two paint stirrers and twine and put it over the grave. "Damn shame," he said, and walked into the house leaving me to wonder if death had somehow changed my father a little for the better. Not likely, I thought. Not likely.

That night I slept on the ground next to the grave. When I woke up Mrs. Hicks was holding a handful of lilacs. "I heard what happened," she said, and tied the lilacs onto Sissy Jupe's cross with a purple ribbon.

For the first time I noticed that she didn't lift her feet up when she walked as if they were too heavy for her legs. I wondered how many other things I missed seeing and didn't know it.

"Can we talk?" Bootsie was holding a hair-do magazine, so I knew she wanted a haircut.

In the bathroom she sat on the toilet with a towel on her lap while I cut the ends of her hair and gave her thick bangs to hide her cowlick. Neither of us spoke, but when she stood-up, she said, "Thanks," and before I had time to reply she was preening in the mirror and begging me to go to Tull's Drugstore.

Then, without waiting for my answer, she fluffed her hair with her fingers, took two quarters out of the Wampum box, and said, "Think anyone'll notice?"

Well, we didn't get any farther than the living room when she got her first compliment. My mother was on the sofa reading the latest issue of LIFE magazine.

"Beautiful," she swooned. "You look just like Patty Duke."

After this, Bootsie walked with her head just a little bit higher than usual and looked around every once in a while to see if anyone was admiring her new look.

Mrs. Benson was coming out of Tull's as we were going in.

"Aren't you stylish?" Bootsie took the question as a backhanded compliment, so she fluffed her hair for the umpteenth time and said, "Thanks."

Inside we ordered root-beer floats. When they arrived Bootsie glanced over her shoulders to make sure no one was within earshot. "To blood sisters," she said, and handed me a bus schedule. "Only three thousand eighty-eight days until you're eighteen, then we can be together forever."

"To us," I said, and we toasted again.

The next morning I talked to Sissy Jupe to make sure he understood I was leaving and that leaving and deserting are not the same thing, and I would not desert him, no matter what. After this I put Mama Cope's tissue snowflake and my red stone in Bootsie's drawer; and when I was sure they were safe I pressed a sprig of lilac from Sissy Jupe's cross between two pieces of wax paper and slid it, and my arrowhead, in a sock. Just then Carole showed up.

"What are you doing?"

I dropped to my knees and pushed the sock under my bed. "Lost something."

Moments later I was in the dining room and smelled chocolate.

I turned around. That's when I saw the white bag and I wanted to tell Carole to throw it in the trash, but she popped a Kiss in her mouth and said, "Daddy said you'd be jealous," and ran out of the room.

Later that afternoon I visited Sissy Jupe one last time. Then I went inside to find my mother. She was ironing.

"Need anything at the grocery store?"

"Milk," she said, and handed me a dollar. She paused for a long moment, then she signaled me to sit down and she continued. "Nothing worth having comes easy . . . nothing." She paused again, then she talked about my father's hard birth and my hard childhood and how, when she married him she thought she could make him happy, but he wasn't happy and none of it was my fault, but "Thank God at least he's trying."

I nodded. It was the best I could do.

I was upstairs when I heard her singing, "Pack up your troubles in your old kit bag and smile, smile, smile . . . ." and I got my sock from under the bed. Carole was nowhere around when I tiptoed downstairs and put the dollar for milk on the dining room table.

When I got outside I looked up. Bootsie had taken the

new screen out of our bedroom window and was waving at me with both hands, crying. I took a deep breath to give me strength. Then I signed: Three thousand eighty-seven days.

"What are you doing?" It was Sarah and Jean Ann. They were wearing their Indian costumes and high-heeled shoes made out of plastic.

"Nothing," I said, and turned towards the highway and kept walking.

Questions for a Deeper Understanding

1. What is the meaning of the story's title?

2. How do setting and characterization work together to reinforce the events of the story? Can you find a pattern at work here?

3. What is the dominant tone of the story and does it give us some important insights into the author's feelings about her childhood?

4. The story is told in a straightforward chronological manner. Does this work for you? Why or why not?

5. Identify some key traits of the main character. How well do these traits serve her throughout the story?

6. How does the kindness of others force Betsy to re-evaluate what she "knows" about human nature?

7. What is the significance of the scene in the woods where Betsy has a vision?

8. In what way(s) does Betsy's sisterly bond with Bootsie have an impact on the outcome of the story?

9. Explain the significance of the scene where Carole is kicked out of the family car.

10. What comment does the story make about children's ability to have a full voice in society?

Made in the USA
Charleston, SC
28 September 2014